New Social Movements, Class, and the Environment

New Social Movements, Class,
and the Environment:
A Case Study of Greenpeace Canada

By

John-Henry Harter

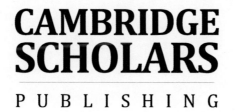

CAMBRIDGE
SCHOLARS
PUBLISHING

New Social Movements, Class, and the Environment:
A Case Study of Greenpeace Canada,
by John-Henry Harter

This book first published 2011

Cambridge Scholars Publishing

12 Back Chapman Street, Newcastle upon Tyne, NE6 2XX, UK

British Library Cataloguing in Publication Data
A catalogue record for this book is available from the British Library

ISBN (10): 1-4438-2863-7, ISBN (13): 978-1-4438-2863-5

TABLE OF CONTENTS

ACKNOWLEDGEMENTS

Thanks to Mark Leier for his support, encouragement, and also some serious editing over the years. As well special thanks to Lee-Anne Clarke for years of listening to different versions of this book back when it was still an idea for my Masters thesis. Without belaboring the point I can not stress that the amount of proofreading, editing, support, and typing, Lee-Anne provided was essential, however her encouragement and partnership were priceless. This book may have been done sooner but the process would not have been as rewarding without our children, Laura, John, Theresa-Anne and Linda. Transitioning from thesis to book has taken so long that Laura now has a son James, who I hope will someday read his grandpa's book. To them I give my thanks and love. Amanda was equally committed to proofreading, editing, and long debates on the nature of class at the onset of this project. Thanks also to the late Ian Dyck and to Gary Teeple who were both on my original thesis committee. I also must thank Willow Reichelt, who agreed to proofread this book at the last possible minute.

Funding in the form of Graduate Fellowships from Simon Fraser University helped me write the original thesis. Portions of this book appeared as an article in *Labour/Le Travail* and I thank them for permission to use it.

INTRODUCTION

On 30 November 1999, in Seattle, Washington, an explosion of outrage against globalization led to massive protest against the World Trade Organization and its millennial round of talks.[1] For the first time in decades, an American city was brought to a standstill by the mobilization of left-wing forces. While remarkable in its own right, the "Battle in Seattle" was significant for the enormous presence of the organized working class. The working class mobilized in force, with over 50,000 trade unionists coming to the city to protest the WTO. Alongside these unionists were new social movement activists from, among others, the student, environmental, and feminist movements. A popular theme written on one of the thousands of placards was "Teamsters and Turtles together at last," signifying the coming together of workers and environmentalists geographically, if not entirely ideologically.[2] While the majority of the labour march did not converge directly on the WTO site, thousands of workers did and it was the size and scope of the labour presence that helped bring so much attention to the protest. The protest in Seattle demonstrated the power of a convergence of class, environmental, and other new social movement politics, while hinting at the inherent difficulties of such a union. This was encouraging and a bright spot in the struggle for social justice to mark the end of the twentieth century.

The "Battle in Seattle" illustrates that the divide between working class and identity politics is not unbridgeable. However, if one believed all the euphoric claims in the days after Seattle, it would seem the collapse of capitalism had occurred on the city streets. While I am loathe to dispel this idea it does need to be put into context. The whole force of the labour march did not converge with the other activists who had shut down the WTO earlier in the day. Alexander Cockburn, a writer for *The Nation*, notes that the legions of labour did not show up for the confrontation in

---

[1] For a thorough account of Seattle from a variety of perspectives, see *Monthly Review*, 52:3 (2000); C.Pearson, "Peaceful in Seatle," *Our Times*, 19 (December/ January 1999); Alexander Cockburn, Jeffery St.Clair, and Alan Sekula, *5 Days That Shook the World: Seattle and Beyond* (London 2000).
[2] Placard as seen by author, 30 November 1999 Seattle Washington. Also documented in John Charlton, "Talking Seattle," *International Socialism*, 86, (2000), 10.

front of the WTO meetings. He wonders what could have happened if they had and fantasizes that it would have been, a humiliation for imperial power of historic proportions, like the famous scene the Wobblies organized to greet Woodrow Wilson after the Seattle general strike had been broken in 1919 – workers and their families lining the streets block after block, standing in furious silence as his motorcade passed by.[3]

Yet Cockburn's analogy misses a very important point. The Wobblies were lining up in the streets after an historic defeat. The marchers in Seattle of 1999 won an historic victory. They shut down a meeting of the world's representatives of capital and the state and they did it in the belly of the beast: the last remaining super power in the world, the United States of America. It is perhaps more correct to see this as a beginning, not an end.

Taking the idea of not just understanding history but changing it, I set out with hundreds of others from Vancouver to join the struggle against the WTO. I went as a member of my union, the Teaching Support Staff Union based at Simon Fraser University, along for the ride with a busload of teachers from the British Columbia Teachers Federation. I attended the labour rally held a number of blocks from the site of the WTO, where the police were at a standoff with the protesters. Much like Cockburn stated, the more than 50,000 at the labour march did not storm the barricades of the police lines. However, the streets between the labour rally and the site of the action were devoid of cars, deserted except for protesters going back and forth. The city was shut down at its core and the left controlled the streets. This was no small feat. As well, while the labour rally was in progress, I managed to make the walk between the two sites in a matter of minutes, as did thousands of others who left the labour rally to join the protest. The Battle in Seattle was shored up by thousands of teamsters, nurses, sheet metal workers, teachers, longshore workers, and at least a handful of university teaching assistants. This is important in that it really was a convergence of new social movements and what some have deemed an old social movement, the working class.

Having a perspective on Seattle is important. Capitalism was not overthrown that day. While the majority of the labour march did not converge on the WTO site thousands did and it was the size and scope of the labour presence that brought so much attention to the protest. One lesson from Seattle was that it demonstrated that working class issues can transcend "narrow economic interests", while it also shows the limits of a labour movement not controlled by a militant, class-conscious rank and file. In addition, it shows how crucial it is to unite class and environmental

---

[3] Alexander Cockburn, "Trade Wars, Trade Truths" *The Nation,* 20, (1999).

and other new social movement politics while suggesting how difficult it will be. The protests against the WTO in Seattle while providing some instructive lessons about workers and new social movements exercising the political power of protest, the day also brings up some serious questions. Why were teamsters and turtles apart in the first place? When did the gulf between new social movements and the working class begin? What were the causes of this split and can they be remedied?

In a study comparing new social movements and old social movements, specifically unions, William K. Carroll and R.S. Ratner note that, "in the social scientific literature of recent years, unions have often been interpreted as social organizations bereft of transformative potential."[4] Since Seattle it has become almost axiomatic in the analysis of anti-globalization protest to lay the blame of any failures, perceived or real, within the anti-globalization movement on organized labour. Often only organized labour's faults and the problems of working class organizations have been examined. For example, in a recent article on the mass mobilization against the Quebec City Summit, Kevin MacKay argues, "much of the conflict between labour and newer social movement groups can be attributed to the conservative, bureaucratized structure of unions."[5] While union bureaucracy is an important area of study and has engendered much debate within labour history, it is too easy to blame organized labour and its bureaucracy for the tensions between itself and other social movements.[6] While Greenpeace is an older, and more bureaucratic, expression of new social movements than the affinity based, anarchistic leaning, anti-globalization movement it does not negate the fact that new social movements need to look at themselves as a whole with a critical eye. John

---

[4]William K. Carroll and R.S. Ratner, "Old Unions and New Social Movements," *Labour/Le Travail*, 35 (Spring 1995), 195.

[5]Kevin MacKay, "Solidarity and Symbolic Protest: Lessons for Labour from the Quebec City Summit of the Americas," *Labour/Le Travail*, 50 (Fall 2002), 22.

[6] On labour bureaucracy see, Mark Leier, *Red Flags and Red Tape: The making of a labour bureaucracy* (Toronto, 1995). On how labour bureaucracy operates and the consequences see, Paul Buhle, *Taking care of business : Samuel Gompers, George Meany, Lane Kirkland, and the Tragedy of American Labor* (New York: Monthly Review Press, 1999). For a slightly different but related debate on labour aristocracy see, Michael Piva, "The Aristocracy of the English Working Class: Help for an Historical Debate in Difficulties" *Histoire sociale/Social History* 7, 14 (1974) Eric Hobsbawm "Debating the Labour Aristocracy" and "The Aristocracy of Labour Reconsidered" *Worlds of Labour: Further Studies in the History of Labour* (London 1984) Richard Price, "The Segmentation of Work and the Labour Aristocracy" *Labour/Le Travail* 17 (Spring 1986): 267-72

Bellamy Foster argues that it is both "the narrow conservationist thrust of most environmentalism in the United States" and the "unimaginative business union response of organized labour" that is the problem when attempting to form coalitions.[7] This book addresses the environmental side of the equation. Business unionism, or social unionism for that matter, is not above reproach. However, the environmental movement is seldom held up to the same scrutiny as the labour movement when discussing the split between labour and environmentalists. Therefore, instead of reprising the labour bureaucracy debates, my focus is on new social movements and how they relate to the working-class in actual campaigns. What, historically, has the relationship been between new social movements and organized labour? How have the structure, composition, and actions of new social movements contributed to the relations between workers and new social movements?

In order to address these questions, this book explores the history of Greenpeace Canada from 1971 to 2010 and its relationship to the working-class. I chose Greenpeace for two main reasons: it has become a brand name for environmentalism and it was formed at the beginning of the era of new social movements. I will examine Greenpeace's structure, personnel, and class origins of its leadership to better understand its actions. I will also look at two of its most famous actions: its opposition to the seal hunt, and its actions against forestry in British Columbia. I also examine a lesser-known Greenpeace campaign against its own workers who were forming a union in Toronto. While a case study of one organization in one social movement cannot test the claims of all new social movements or new social movement literature, I hope to provoke questions about new social movements and the theories that often make assertions about the nature of social movements without historical reference or case studies.[8] In this way I will provide a different lens

---

[7] John Bellamy Foster, "The Limits of Environmentalism without Class: Lessons From the Ancient Forest Struggle in the Pacific Northwest" in *The Stuggle for Ecological Democracy: Envrionmental Justice Movements in the United States* ed. Daniel Faber (New York: The Guilford Press1998) p.189.

[8] William K. Carroll notes that "there has been a dearth of available texts that probe the meaning of movements in a distinctly Canadian context." William K. Carroll, "Introduction," *Organizing Dissent: Contemporary Social Movements in Theory and Practice* (Victoria: Garamond Press, 1992), 3. Laurie Adkin also remarks on this lack of actual case studies, stating "A reader of 'orthodox Marxist' versus 'post Marxist' interpretations of trade unions to radical social change, of the historical meaning of the new social movements, cannot but be struck by the general absence of analyses of actually existing social movements. New Social

through which to look at new social movement actions and helps reinsert class into the discourse around social movements through case study of specific environmental campaigns.

I outline the history of Greenpeace and its place as a new social movement in Chapter one. In order to understand the ideas and themes discussed in the book, Chapter one also looks at the history and theory of new social movements. Chapter two explores Greenpeace by examining its structure, personnel, and class in order to better understand the ideology behind the actions of Greenpeace. Chapter three looks at one of Greenpeace's most famous actions, its opposition to the seal hunt, to see the effects of its ideology on its actions. Chapter four looks at Greenpeace's actions against forestry in British Columbia. In Chapter five I examine how Greenpeace deals with its own workers in Toronto to see how it has dealt with internal labour issues. In Chapter six, I look at two of the main claims on which Greenpeace, and new social movement theorists as a whole, base their politics: first, that working class movements are obsolete; and second, that the only agents of progressive social change are new social movements acting in the interests of all humanity. Greenpeace and new social movements generally claim their interests are universal and beyond the concerns of class, yet this is contradicted by their actions. By using Greenpeace as a case study, I explore the contradiction between new social movement theory and action that occurs when dealing with issues of class. The questions raised by the Battle of Seattle should not be answered abstractly. If there is to be a successful movement against globalization and against the forces of capitalism moving that agenda, then one has to look at the history that has stopped that movement from being successful in the past. In that way this book contributes not only to a better understanding of the history of Greenpeace, but also of how new social movements have historically dealt with class and how it could be done differently in the future.

Movements and unions have been much theorized about, but little studied from 'ground level.'" *The Politics of Sustainable Development: Citizens, Unions and the Corporations* (Montreal: Black Rose Books, 1998), xiii.

CHAPTER ONE

GREENPEACE AND NEW SOCIAL MOVEMENT THEORY

Thirty years have passed since Vancouver's *Georgia Straight* carried the one word headline: "Greenpeace." The accompanying article outlined plans for the first voyage of what was then called the "Don't Make a Wave Committee":

> Saturday the group formalized plans to send a ship they'll rename *Greenpeace* into the Amchitka area before the next test. Greenpeace is an ambitious and maybe impossible project, but so is anything that tries to promote a sane approach to the world we live in.[1]

This was the beginning of Greenpeace, a prototypical new social movement. Started as the "Don't Make a Wave Committee" in order to oppose American nuclear testing, it was incorporated as Greenpeace in 1972. The original Greenpeace document consisted of a slip of paper noting the change of name stapled to a photocopy of the standard structure for societies as directed by the BC government regulations in the Society Act.[2] The first campaign consisted of a crew of twelve men who chartered the now famous boat *Phyllis Cormack* on 15 September 1971 to "bear witness" to the nuclear test on the island Amchitka in the North West Pacific. The blast at Amchitka was not prevented, but Greenpeace declared the action a victory since the American government never used the

---

[1] *Georgia Straight,* 18-25 February 1970.

[2] The name Greenpeace apparently originated when a Don't Make a Wave Committee meeting was ended by saying "Peace." Social worker Bill Darnell responded "Make it a Green Peace." Mark Warford, ed. *Greenpeace: Witness, Twenty-Five Years on the Environmental Front Line* (London: Andre Deutsh, 1996), 9; Michael Brown and John May, *The Greenpeace Story* (Scarborough Ontario: Prentice-Hall Canada, 1989), 9; Robert Hunter, *Warriors of the Rainbow: A Chronicle of the Greenpeace Movement* (New York: Holt, Rinehart and Winston, 1979), 7; and Karl and Dona Sturmanis, *The Greenpeace Book* (Vancouver: Orca Sound Publications, 1978).

Amchitka site again and because of the extensive media coverage
Greenpeace received.[3] Greenpeace has grown exponentially since its
beginnings in Vancouver and its first campaign opposing nuclear testing: it
now has international offices, a wide breadth of involvement in the
ecology movement, and international media exposure.

The development of Greenpeace was not unique and was similar to
other groups that fall under the rubric of new social movements. New
social movements were the products of the break-up of the New Left at the
end of the 1960s. The New Left fractured into a multitude of single issue
groups representing the peace movement, the environmental movement,
the student movement, the women's movement, and the gay liberation
movement.[4] The creation of these single issue groups were seen by some
academics as an indication that "old" social action groups, especially the
"old left," composed of workers and unions, were incapable of addressing
these issues. It was in this fractured socio-political context that the 1970s
saw an explosion of new social movement theory and activism.[5] Before

---

[3] For comment on the media savvy of Greenpeace see Stephen Dale, *McLuhan's
Children: the Greenpeace Message and the Media* (Toronto: Between the Lines,
1990).

[4] In many ways the definitive book on the New Left, one which encompasses all
the formations on the left, remains to be written. One prevalent theme in the
literature on the New Left is the reduction of the scope of the New Left to a study
of white middle class students. In his chapter on the "Beginnings of the New
Left," Milton Cantor notes that the participants were, "mostly white, well-
educated, suburban youth of similar backgrounds." Milton Cantor, *The Divided
Left: American Radicalism 1900-1975* (New York: Hill and Wang, 1978),183.
James O'Brien states at the beginning of his study of the New Left that, "One self-
imposed limitation of this study which should be made clear is that it is a study of
white students." James O'Brien, *The Development of a New Left in the United
States, 1960-1965,* Ph.D. Thesis, University of Wisconsin, 1971, ii. One American
book of primary documents separates the documents on the 1960s into a section
on Black Liberation and a section on the New Left. Immanuel Wallerstein and Paul
Starr, eds.. *The University Crisis Reader: Volume I and II* (New York: Random
House, 1971). The term New Left appears to only apply to white middle class
activists. This ignores the important contributions to the Left by Blacks organized
in the Southern Nonviolent Coordinating Committee (SNCC) and then the Black
Panther Party; the white working class participation in labour struggles and grass
roots anti-imperialist groups (for example, the George Jackson Brigade); black
students organized under Black Student Alliance umbrella groups; and Native
Americans organized in the American Indian Movement (AIM). None of those
groups are usually referred to as New Left.
[5] New social movement theory was first put forward by French sociologist Alaine
Touraine. See Alaine Touraine, *The Voice and Eye: An Analysis of Social Movements*

Greenpeace can be thoroughly examined as a new social movement, the question of what defines new social movements needs to be explored further. New social movement theorists have put forward a variety of models to explain exactly how new social movements work in theory and practice.[6]

The roots of new social movement theory can be traced to the attempt by Marxists to explain different social formations within capitalism in the post-war era and the supposed "failure" of the working class in the pre- and post-war periods. Particularly influenced by Herbert Marcuse and Louis Althusser, sociologists began to work on theories that embraced the idea of a "new working class" as a revolutionary agent.[7] Pressed to explain

---

(Cambridge: Cambridge University Press, 1981). Ernesto Laclau and Chantal Mouffe are often associated with the first works on new social movement theory, however, Touraine's first foray into this field can be traced to his book *The May Movement Revolt and Reform: May 1968 – The Student Rebellion and Workers' Strikes – the Birth of a Social Movement* (New York: Random House, 1971). See also John A. Hannigan, "Alaine Touraine, Manuel Castells and Social Movement Theory: A Critical Appraisal," *The Sociological Quarterly*, 26: 4 (1985): 435-454.

[6] The development of social movement theory has not been uniform. One of the first attempts of American sociologists to understand social movement formation is the collective behavior model. This model puts forward two explanatory models to explain mass movement participation. The first is the normative breakdown thesis which explains movement formation as an irrational response to a sudden societal change. Closely associated with this theory are Neil J. Smelser and Chalmers Johnson. See Neil J. Smelser, *The Theory of Collective Behavior* (New York: Free Press, 1963); and Chalmers Johnson, *Revolutionary Change* (Boston: Little Brown, 1966). The other model argues that it is the group response to relative deprivation that is the impetus for movement formation. Ted Gurr, *Why Men Rebel* (Princeton, N.J.: Princeton University Press, 1970). Resource Mobilization Theory is a more current theory; it is sometimes used instead of, and sometimes in conjunction with, new social movement theory. For articles comparing NSM and RMT see Barry D. Adam, "Post-Marxism and the New Social Movements," *The Canadian Review of Sociology and Anthropology*, 30, (1993), 316-36; and Hannigan, "Alaine Touraine." Resource Mobilization Theory examines how people with shared interests pool their resources – money, skills, labour – to achieve a specific goal. Unlike the collective behaviour model, in this theory the participants are rational actors. The theorist most associated with Resource Mobilization Theory is Charles Tilly. Charles Tilly, *From Mobilization to Revolution* (Reading: Addison-Wesley, 1978); and *As Sociology Meets History*, (New York: Academic Press, 1981).

[7] Canadian sociologist William K. Carroll notes that in Canada the influence of Harold Innis and his staples theory and the adaptation of Marxist theories of uneven development into a hinterland/urban centre model fueled Canadian sociology. Carroll, *Organizing Dissent*, 3-39.

the revolutionary activity of French students, professionals, and petit bourgeoisie in May of 1968, these Marxists began to explore how to account for these activists, and explain their alleged failure of the working class. Althusser shifted the attention of Marxists from the "economic base," or the forces of production in society, to the "superstructure," which is everything else including politics, religion, and culture. He focused on culture, part of the superstructure, in order to explain the development of this new way of struggle and new revolutionary agent. However, Althusser did not completely abandon class, and believed that class was the determinant in the last instance.[8] What the last instance was, or how it was determined, was never fully explained.

The theorist who expanded these ideas into the theory of the "new working class" was French sociologist Alaine Touraine. In *The May Movement Revolt and Reform: May 1968 – the Student Rebellion and Workers' Strikes – the Birth of a Social Movement*, Touraine theorized that a new working class developed out of the current era of capitalism as illustrated by the May Movement. Touraine differed from orthodox Marxism, arguing that modern industrial capitalism had created a new working class. In his opinion this new working class was made up of professionals, not industrial workers. As Touraine puts it, "The main actor in the May movement was not the working class but the totality of those whom we may call the professionals."[9] Since '68 Touraine has become something of a specialist on social movements and has founded the *Centre d'analyse et d'intervention sociologiques* in Paris (CADIS). Touraine has applied his theory of a new working class to the anti-nuclear movement in France and the Solidarity movement in Poland.[10] A major theme in Touraine's analysis is that class relations have changed within modern advanced industrial capitalist society. Within advanced capitalism, Touraine argues, a new relationship between capital and labour is forged where professionals replace traditional workers. This new relationship occurs as professionals become responsible for tending the technologically

---

[8] Louis Althusser, *Lenin and Philosophy and Other Essays*, (London: New Left Books, 1971).

[9] Touraine, *The May Movement*. The debate of where to put the "professionals," or some sections of white collar workers is not new. Karl Kautsky used the term "new middle class" to describe this group in 1899 and the debate ensued from there. On Kautsky and earlier debates around the new middle class see Bob Carter, *Capitalism, Class Conflict, and the New Middle Class* (London: Routledge & Kegan Paul, 1985) particularly the section "The German Debate," 16-31.

[10] Alaine Touraine, *Anti-nuclear Protest: The Opposition to Nuclear Energy in France* (Cambridge: Cambridge University Press, 1983).

sophisticated machinery necessary for advanced capitalist industry. According to Touraine, in May '68, these technicians, civil servants, engineers, researchers, scientists, and students training to be in those professions, formed not only a new social movement but also a new class.

While Touraine's argument appears to explain the events of May '68, there are inconsistencies in the facts he presents and some flaws in his conclusions. For instance, Touraine states that, "The profound unity of the movement was due to the fact that it was no longer fighting a ruling group defending private interests but generalized power over social and cultural life."[11] Touraine's claims of a profound unity are contrary to many other works on May '68.[12] Touraine's theory of a new working class is also questionable. What he is really talking about is the fluidity of an old class, the professional managerial class, exaggerated to explain a whole new social formation reliant more on subtle differences in how capitalism is managed and how the workers relate to the tools of production. This new class argument is premised on the notion that those responsible for tending to the technologically sophisticated capitalist machinery, are different because they tend different machinery. However, although new technology can throw some workers out of work, or create a new craft or trade it does not make a new class. In the printing industry, for example, the change from hand-set type to Linotypes to computers has changed the medium of typography, not the class position of workers in the trade.

Nor does Touraine's analysis explain how his "new working class" automatically displaces the "old" working class or why it should be substituted for already existing class distinctions. When Touraine talks about professionals or managers he does not show why they are not part of the professional managerial class. When he talks about computer technicians, or mechanics who service the new technology, he does not explain why they are not part of the working class. In many ways, Touraine shows instead that that it is possible for the members of the

---

[11] Touraine, *The May Movement*, 58.

[12] For numerous books, from a variety of ideological perspectives, that contradict Touraine's claim of profound unity see: Daniel Cohn-Bendit, *Obsolete Communism: The Left-Wing Alternative*, trans. Arnold Pomerans, (New York: McGraw-Hill Book Company, 1968); Roger Salloch, *In Pursuit of Ideology: The French Student Revolt, May/June 1968* (United States: Massachusetts Institute of Technology, Center for International Studies, 1969); Jean Jacques Servan-Schreiber, *The Spirit of May* trans. Ronald Steel, (New York: McGraw-Hill Book Company, 1968); and Raymond Aron, *The Elusive Revolution: Anatomy of a Student Revolt* trans. Gordon Clough, (New York: Praeger Publishers, 1969).

middle class to achieve class consciousness and band together with the working class.[13]

One question the new social movements arguments fail to address is what happened to the "old working class?" It is still at work, still alienated, and still without ownership of the means of production. Even in May '68 one of the main sites of struggle was the auto factories. In Italy, the huge upsurge in workers' activity was referred to as the "Hot Autumn" of 1969 and continued through to 1974 with workers organizing outside of the mainstream unions and the Communist Party. Groups such as *Lotta Continua* (LC or Continuous Struggle) advocated Council Communism, "believing that workers can make their own decisions regarding how society should be run without any assistance from vanguard parties."[14] At its peak LC had over 50,000 activists and branches in every one of Italy's ninety-four provinces. In Rome alone they had twenty-one neighbourhood offices.[15] Including other autonomous workers groups such as *Potere Operaio* (Workers' Power), *Il Manifesto*, and *Autonomia Operaia* (Workers' Autonomy), the Italian working class movements in the 1970s had millions of members and sympathizers. One example of the size and militancy of the working class at the time was on 9 February 1973 when approximately 500,000 workers marched in Rome. This was the largest gathering of workers since World War II. Their slogans included "Power to the Workers!" and "Factory, School, Community – Our Struggle Is for Power!"[16]

In the United States, the Dodge Revolutionary Union Movement started organizing resistance to the conditions in Detroit auto plants. A wildcat strike against Chrysler at the Detroit Dodge Main Plant inspired many other revolutionary movement groups across Detroit. This eventually led to the formation of the League of Revolutionary Black Workers and then the Black Workers Congress.[17] In Canada, there was a huge upswing in workers' mobilization: one-quarter of job actions after 1900 took place between 1971 and 1975. In 1976, one and a half million

---

[13] Klaus Eder similarly argues that the middle class has a central role in the restructuring of the classes in his book, *The New Politics of Class: Social Movements and Cultural Dynamics in Advanced Societies* (London: Sage, 1993).

[14] George Katsiaficas, *The Subversion of Politics: European Autonomous Social Movements and the Decolonization of Everyday Life* (New Jersey: Humanities Press, 1997), 24.

[15] Katsiaficas, *The Subversion of Politics,* 24.

[16] Katsiaficas, *The Subversion of Politics,* 26.

[17] Dan Georgakas and Marvin Surkin, *Detroit: I Do Mind Dying: A Study in Urban Revolution* (Cambridge, Massachusetts: South End Press 1998).

workers went on strike accounting for 11.6 million person-days lost. Significantly, three out of ten strikes in the 1970s were wildcats. Italy was said to be the only Western country in the world to match Canadian workers' militancy.[18] Within the context of these protests, it is difficult to understand how new social movement theorists could insist that the working class was no longer relevant to social change. Perhaps the real problem was one of identification. The working class has never been homogenous, and in order to gain a clear understanding of the working class it is necessary to go beyond the incomplete and incorrect definition that it is only male, industrial, blue collar workers. However, instead of formulating a more accurate definition of the working class, most new social movement theorists have given up using class as a relevant subject of analysis.

Alberto Melucci, one of the first new social movement theorists, explicitly rejects class as a tool of analysis. "I have gradually abandoned the concept of class relationships," he states. "In systems like contemporary ones, where classes as real social groups are withering away, more appropriate concepts are required."[19] Melucci deserts historical materialism for "slices of experience, past history, and memory."[20] Laurie Adkin, a Canadian sociologist, follows Melucci's abandonment of class as a key social relation and claims that the key to understanding new social movements is grasping that "class identity and culture of a previous era no longer encompass the experiences of enough persons to constitute the core identity of a mass movement for profound social change."[21]

The idea that the working class is dead is premised on false assumptions and an ahistorical view of the composition of the working class. In her book, *A Question of Class*, British socialist Lindsey German details this stereotype as a "classic view of the working class – almost exclusively male, working in heavy industry."[22] She also notes that "total employment in manufacturing industry never, at any time, amounted to one half of the employed population, although it was, until recently the

---

[18] Craig Heron, *The Canadian Labour Movement: A Short History* 2nd edition (Toronto: Lorimer, 1996), 94.

[19] Alberto Melucci, "A Strange Kind of Newness: What's 'New' in New Social Movements?" *New Social Movements: From Ideology to Identity,* Enrique Larana, Hank Johnston, and Joseph R. Gusfield, eds.. (Philadelphia: Temple University Press, 1994), 103.

[20] Melucci, " A Strange Kind," 115.

[21] Adkin, *Sustainable Development,* 10.

[22] Lindsey German, *A Question of Class* (London: Bookmarks, 1996), 24.

largest single sector."[23] Another important point German makes is that service sector jobs are not new or only in fast food restaurants or retail sales. Historically, "transport workers, postal workers, dockers and telecom engineers all fall into the services category. They have always made up a substantial proportion of the workforce even in the heyday of manufacturing."[24] Indeed, when Karl Marx wrote *Capital*, the largest single occupational group was that of domestic workers, largely female and certainly in the service sector.

This is also the case in Canada. The advent of a female, low waged, office clerk occurred over a period of thirty years, from the turn of the century to the 1930s. "Up until the end of the 1910s offices were run by generalist male bookkeepers but by the 1920s they had been replaced by female functionaries with adding machines who had less status, less wages, and monotonously repetitive jobs."[25] The introduction of a deskilled female work force "was part of a massive restructuring of the means of administration."[26] While nominally "white collar" it is only by contrasting these workers against the "classic" male industrial worker that these workers could somehow be seen as middle class. A more accurate identification is "pink collar workers," denoting a largely female job sector that is part of the working class. Bryan Palmer recognizes that, "by 1971 the clerical subsection of white-collar workers was the largest occupational grouping in the country, with over 1.3 million working members."[27] This was not the disappearance of the working class; rather, it was a massive influx in the ranks of the working class. These workers were very far removed from the professional managerial class. A union official coined the term "quiet factories" to describe their workplaces, making the link between the industrial and the non- industrial working class.[28] Far from the working class becoming obsolete, replaced by a "new working class," the reality was and is that some traditionally middle class and professional groups were becoming proletarianized.

---

[23] German, *Class*, 25.

[24] German, *Class*, 29.

[25] Graham S. Lowe, "Mechanization, Feminization and Managerial Control in the Early Twentieth-Century Canadian Office," *On The Job: Confronting the labour process in Canada* Craig Heron and Robert Storey eds. (Kingston and Montreal: McGill-Queen's University Press, 1986), 194.

[26] Lowe, "Mechanization," 179.

[27] Bryan D. Palmer, *Working-Class Experience: Rethinking the History of Canadian Labour, 1800-1991.* 2nd Ed. (Toronto: McClelland and Stewart, 1992), 323.

[28] Palmer, *Working-Class*, 324.

Why do new social movements ignore class despite its obvious existence? How can new social movement theorists and activists ignore the working class mobilizations of the past and present to argue the so-called death of the working class in the 1970s to present? Their argument is directly tied to the idea that the working class can not address issues of identity. The importance of addressing identity has become the most pervasive argument put forward by new social movement theorists to explain why single issue movements or new social movements are more effective tools for organizing in a "post modern" society. Laurie Adkin, for example, cites Chantal Mouffe who writes, "In order that the defense of the interests of workers' interests is not pursued at the cost of the rights of women, immigrants, or consumers, it is necessary to establish an equivalence between these different struggles."[29] This is a very narrow conception of the terms worker and workers' interest. Again, the stereotypical male, white, industrial worker is invoked as a representative of the working class as a whole. Mouffe, and in turn Adkin, are creating a dichotomy where one does not naturally exist. Of course not all women are workers but the way Mouffe frames the issue, none of them are. She also presupposes that women, immigrants, and consumers of all classes have something inherently more important in common than do working class men and women; she places identity above the interests of the working class.[30] The new social movement theorists use the notion of diversity within the working class to claim that it means fragmentation, yet this is not inevitable nor is it readily apparent.

This theory's disassociation from class in favour of identity has been put forward as post-Marxism, post-structuralism, post-modernism, and more recently "radical democracy." Put succinctly, the argument is that

> new social movements are based not in material interests but in the discursive practices that construct new political subjects, create new political spaces in which to act , and may ultimately lead people to rethink what we mean by community, or power, or reason, or power, or consciousness or energy, or security, or development or democracy.[31]

Ernesto Laclau, a leading theorist on social movements, in his 1990 book New *Reflections on the Revolution of Our Time*, agrees:

---

[29] Chantal Mouffe, cited in Adkin, *Sustainable Development*, 10.

[30] It is ironic that Mouffe includes "consumer" in her list of important identities as it is only in capitalism that the role of consumer would be considered an identity in the same way as gender and race.

[31] Carroll, Organizing Dissent, 8.

The demands of a lesbian group, a neighbors' association, or a black self-defense group are therefore all situated on the same ontological level as working class demands. In this way the absence of a global emancipation of humanity allows the constant expansion and diversification of concrete emancipatory struggles.[32]

This focus on discourse reduces class to an identity that is not differentiated from neighborhood associations or self-defence classes. This reduction through equivalence makes the retreat from class complete. Laclau does not identify the class nature of the groups, their goals, purpose, or statements of principles and yet somehow these groups' demands are seen as no different than working class demands. If this is the case, then demanding a stop sign at an intersection in your neighborhood is revolutionary. It is this exclusion of any class analysis that seems to have predominated in the thinking of Greenpeace and has become pervasive in new social movements on the whole. Occasionally members of the working class may be useful allies but that is the extent of it.

There is dissent against the theories put forward by new social movement theorists. Those dissenting argue that the intellectual move away from so-called "foundational"[33] narratives to explore the fractured identities and multiplicity of experience characterized by postmodernism and framed in new social movements represents a retreat from class and is essentially re-framing bourgeois liberalism in a different guise.[34] Ellen Meiksins Wood identifies this trend within the left that dissociates politics from class and socialist politics from the interests and struggles of the working class. Those who subscribe to this theoretical turn, Wood asserts, are really only arguing for an extension of bourgeois democratic forms.[35] Wood's assertion applies to the new social movement theorists who argue that class is irrelevant and thus, theoretically, erases class stratification through discourse. Similarly, according to Melucci, "the goal is to render power visible not to challenge it because conflicts have no winners, but they may produce innovation, modernization and reform."[36] At its core,

---

[32] Ernesto Laclau, *New Reflections on the Revolution of Our Time* (London: Verso, 1990), 216.

[33] See Joan Scott, "The Evidence of Experience," *Critical Inquiry*, 17 (1991), 773-797.

[34] See Bryan Palmer, *Descent into Discourse: The Reification of Language and the Writing of Social History* (Philadelphia: Temple University Press, 1990) for a critique of this trend and Scott, "The Evidence of Experience," for an example of it.

[35] Ellen Meiksins Wood, *The Retreat from Class: A New "True" Socialism* (London: Verso, 1986).

[36] Melucci, *Nomads of the Present*, 77-78.

the new social movement argument is really about modest reforms to capitalism. By deeming class struggle irrelevant, capitalism is never challenged, just altered to allow access to a few more groups. Thus class struggle is contained and the hegemony of capitalism maintained.

In their attempt to discredit both class as an explanatory tool and the working class as a revolutionary agent, new social movement theorists create a straw argument against Marx. New social movement theory rests on the idea that there is a discontinuity in capitalism; while class once mattered, it is not important now in the post modern era. However, this discontinuity does not exist. As Wood points out, the logic of capitalism – accumulation, commodification, profit-maximization, and competition – has not changed: it has only adapted to current conditions. As Wood states,

> If we have been seeing something new since the 1970s it's not a major discontinuity in capitalism but, on the contrary, capitalism itself reaching maturity. It may be that we're seeing the first real efforts of capitalism as a comprehensive system.[37]

Wood is arguing that rather than a discontinuity in capitalism we are seeing a realization of capitalism's goal, a comprehensive capitalist system.

In her book *The Politics of Sustainable Development,* Laurie Adkin criticizes Ellen Meiksins Wood for privileging workers in the anti-capitalist struggle as the "people who are the direct objects of class exploitation."[38] Adkin claims this "reflects an old dichotomous way of thinking on the left in which all practice is either labelled 'social democratic reformist' or 'revolutionary.'"[39] What Adkin overlooks is that the people who are the direct objects of capitalist exploitation are, and can only be, the working class. This does not mean, as Adkin claims, that the women's struggle, or anti-racism, or any other struggle against oppression should wait until after the class struggle: rather, they are part of the class struggle. As capitalism attempts to divide the working class along other lines, the class struggle must include the entirety of the working class and resist divisions.

---

[37] Ellen Meiksins Wood, "Modernity, Postmodernity, or Capitalism?" *Monthly Review* 48: 3 (July-August 1996), 37.

[38] Adkin, *Sustainable Development*, 7.

[39] Adkin, *Sustainable Development*, 7.

CHAPTER TWO

GREENPEACE, DEMOCRACY, AND CLASS

The structure of Greenpeace is important to investigate in order to understand how decisions are made and whether there is a potential for class issues to be raised within the group. It is also necessary to analyze the class position of those within Greenpeace in order to open up the question of how their class may affect the politics of Greenpeace. Illustrating the middle class biographies of new social movement actors is not new; however there has been little analysis of how the class composition of new social movements affects their actual campaigns. I use the theory of the professional managerial class in this chapter in an attempt to understand how class influenced the ideology and actions of Greenpeace.

The theory of the professional managerial class allows an understanding of the motivations and the class interests of Greenpeace and makes explicable their ideology and actions. The term professional managerial class best describes the class position of Greenpeace officials. Barbara and John Ehrenrich identify the professional managerial class as "consisting of salaried menial workers who do not own the means of production and whose major function in the social division of labor may be described broadly as the reproduction of capitalist culture and capitalist class relations."[1] This is a useful starting point. However, Erik Olin Wright argues that the Ehrenreichs' professional managerial class model is functionalist and falters as a complete analysis because it defines the professional managerial class by its function of reproducing capitalist culture and class relations but does not adequately consider the relationship to the means of production. Instead, Wright asserts that the professional managerial class occupies contradictory class locations: between the bourgeoisie and the proletariat, in the case of supervisors and managers; and between the petit bourgeoisie and the working class, in the case of semi-autonomous employees. A synthesis of these two analyses

---

[1] Barbara and John Ehrenreich, "The Professional-Managerial Class," *Radical America* 11: 2 (1977): 13.

provides an excellent definition of the professional managerial class. The Ehrenreichs' functional analysis is important as it clearly states the role of the professional managerial class, while the contradictory class locations analysis is necessary as it explains the relationship of the professional managerial class to the means of production. The term professional managerial class is preferable to middle class, new middle class, or other vague terms because it more carefully describes who comprises this class. Alex Callincos helps expand the understanding of the professional managerial class by explaining Stanley Arnowitz's idea that the professional managerial class is not static.

> It means the new middle class is not hermetically sealed off from other classes. At the top it shades off into the higher echelons of management and administration, which are effectively part of the ruling class. At the lower end it merges into the working class.[2]

The professional managerial class was the predominant constituency with Greenpeace from the beginning and bears more scrutiny than it has been previously accorded.

Among the founding members of Greenpeace, and those who would become the most well known initially, were those who went out on the first Greenpeace action to stop the atom bomb tests at Amchitka. The group was composed of three journalists: Robert Hunter, from the *Vancouver Sun;* Ben Metcalfe, a theatre critic for the CBC; and Bob Cummings from the *Georgia Straight.* The journalists were there as members of the protest group, though their role as media personalities would greatly enhance their media coverage. The other crew members were Jim Bohlen, a forest products researcher; Patrick Moore, a graduate student at UBC; Bill Darnell, a social worker; Dr. Lyle Thruston, a medical practitioner; Terry Simmons, a cultural geographer; and Richard Fineberg, a political science professor.[3] All of these men fit within the professional managerial class as semi-autonomous employees, with the exception perhaps of the grad student, who was a professional manager in training so to speak, and the doctor, who depending upon his practice could have been in the supervisor, manager role of the professional managerial class. The class composition of the executive of Greenpeace changed little over the years. In 1994, the board of directors for

---

[2] Alex Callinicos, "The 'New Middle Class' and Socialist Politics," *International Socialism* 2:20 (1985): 104.

[3] This list of members of the original crew is complied from Brown and May, *The Greenpeace Story,* 11; and Hunter, *Warriors,* 16-17. See also *Vancouver Sun* "Greenpeace sailors ready to face the test" 15 September 1971, 43.

Greenpeace Canada were Olivier Deleuze, an agronomic engineer; Joanne Dufay, a health professional; Harvey MacKinnon, a fundraising consultant; Janet Patterson, an accountant; Trudie Richards, a university professor; Steve Sawyer, an Executive Director of Greenpeace International; and Steve Shrybman, a lawyer.[4]

The professional managerial class base of Greenpeace's officers is consistent with the new social movement theory literature that often embraces the middle class as the agent of change in society.[5] Theorists have tended to argue that new social movements have displaced the working class as the agent of positive social change in society.[6] The Ehrenreichs argue the class interests of the professional managerial class are achieved by a "PMC radicalism" which,

> emerges out of PMC class interests, which include the PMC's interest in extending its technological and cultural superiority over the working class. Thus the possibility exists in the PMC for the emergence of what may at first sight seem to be a contradiction in terms: anti-working class radicalism. This possibility finds its fullest expression in the PMC radical's recurring vision of a technocratic socialism, a socialism in which the bourgeoisie has been replaced by bureaucrats, planners, and experts of various sorts.[7]

The point is not that anti-working class radicalism is inevitable nor does it mean that groups like Greenpeace are inherently regressive. The point is that the possibility for anti-working class radicalism exists within the professional managerial class and that new social movements made up largely of the professional managerial class could easily fall into such behaviour. The possibility of anti-working class radicalism is ignored

---

[4] Greenpeace Annual Review, 1994.

[5] On new social movement and the middle class see: Russell Dalton and Manfred Kuechler, eds. *Challenging the Political Order*. (New York: Oxford University Press, 1990); Klaus Eder, "Green Politics and the New Class," *Political Studies*, 37: 2, (1989), 205-223; Jurgen Habermas, *The Theory of Communicative Action*, Vol. 2 (Boston: Beacon Halfmann, Jost, 1987); and Herbert Kitschelt, "'New Social Movements in West Germany and the United States," *Political Power and Social Theory*, 5: 310, (1985).

[6] Klaus Eder, "The New Social Movements: Moral Crusades, Political Pressure Groups, or Social Movements?" *Social Research* 52: 4 (1985): .869-890; Claus Offe, "New Social Movements: Challenging the Boundaries of Institutional Politics" *Social Research* 52: 4 (1985): 831-832; Warren Magnusson and R. Walker, "De-Centring the State: Political Theory and Canadian Political Economy," *Studies in Political Economy* 26, (1988), 37-71.

[7] Barbara and John Ehrenreich, as quoted in Callinicos, "Socialist Politics," 109.

when new social movements are painted as acting in a benevolent, altruistic, and classless manner. This idea co-exists with the idea that new social movements are inherently more inclusive and democratic than old social movements. While I cannot address the broader claims of classlessness of new social movements, I can show how these assumptions play out in specific campaigns.

It is important to look at the organizational structure of Greenpeace as well as the class composition of its leadership to see how different voices are heard within the organization. This helps us see if working class issues could be addressed within the structure of Greenpeace. This is particularly important because inclusion and democratic structures are given much importance in new social movements' theory.[8] Lawrence Wilde notes that new social movements emphasize "radical democratic internal structures and processes, including rotation of offices, open meetings, and limitation of rewards."[9] Greenpeace appeared to reflect these ideas in their structure. According to Robert Hunter, one of the founders of Greenpeace, by 1977:

> Virtually anybody could set themselves up as a Greenpeace office, taking more or less full credit for all the achievements to date, and appoint himself or herself to a position, using no formulas more elaborate than the one we had used ourselves in Vancouver: simply, you get a bunch of your friends in a room and proclaim yourselves.[10]

The founders of Greenpeace believed that their lack of formal structures allowed Greenpeace to create a group that was non-hierarchical, decentralized, and democratic.[11] However Greenpeace was not organized using alternative structures. In fact, it was structureless. Decisions in the fledgling Greenpeace were made on an *ad hoc* basis. There were no structural mechanisms for decision making. While this likely suited the small nature of the group at the founding, it created the basis for a fundamentally undemocratic organization in which decisions were made by a small group of people, predominately men from the professional

---

[8]Carl Boggs, *Social Movements and Political Power* (Philadelphia 1986); Alberto Melucci, *Nomads of the Present: Social Movements and Individual Needs in Contemporary Society* (Philadelphia 1989); Alan Scott, *Ideology and the New Social Movements* (London 1990); and Joachim Hirsch, "The Crisis of Fordism, Transformations of the 'Keynesian' Security State and the New Social Movements." *Research in Social Movements, Conflicts and Change*, 10: 43-55.

[9] Lawrence Wilde, "Class Analysis and the Politics of New Social Movements," *Capital and Class*. 42, (1990), 55.

[10] Hunter, *Warriors*, 365.

[11] See Hunter, *Warriors*.

managerial class.[12] Again, this itself does not prove anti-working-class bias but does suggest inclusivity was problematic.

It sounds paradoxical to argue that a lack of structure can impede democracy and exclude some voice. However, Jo Freeman, a feminist writing on the women's movement, argues that to strive for a "structureless" group is as useful and as deceptive, as to aim for an "objective" news story, "value-free" social science, or a "free" economy and that attempting to operate a structureless group "does not prevent the formation of informal structures, but only formal ones" and the "structurelessness becomes a way of making power."[13] Freeman critiques structurelessness for its informal networks that create an invisible power structure that prevents democratic member participation. This is the anti-democratic system that Greenpeace operated with for years. Greenpeace lacked even the semblance of internal democracy for close to a decade. According to Robert Hunter at the beginning in 1972, "Instead of a board we had two 'interim chairmen,' we had not had any general meetings."[14] This undemocratic state of affairs did not improve with time. Until at least 1977 anybody could create a Greenpeace group and appoint themselves to positions of power without any structure whatsoever. As Hunter explained, "you get a bunch of your friends in a room and proclaim yourselves."[15] This contradicts the idea of participatory democracy as it leaves an elite group to proclaim themselves the leaders and asks the rest of the "membership" to follow. There are no democratic structures set up to deal with issues or to make decisions. If the leaders proclaim themselves, how are they accountable? How are their decisions reached? Who gets a say and who doesn't? None of these questions can be adequately addressed in such a structureless formation and this contradicts the idea of grassroots, active, democratic, membership driven organization.[16] More to the point of this study is how the membership of Greenpeace was insular and

---

[12] Jo Freeman, "The Tyranny of Structurelessness" in *Untying the Knot – Feminism, Anarchism & Organization* (London: Dark Star Press and Rebel Press, 1984).

[13] Freeman, 'The Tyranny,"

[14] Hunter, *Warriors*, 123.

[15] Hunter, *Warriors*, 365.

[16] This is not a criticism of alternative structures, such as consensus based decision making, participatory democracy, or power sharing, used in many feminist and anarchist organizations. It is specifically a critique of structurelessness the type of which was occurring within Greenpeace for at least their first decade of existence and the problems this lack of structure can create.

comprised primarily of the professional managerial class. This made it difficult not only to influence decisions within Greenpeace but to understand how decisions were made within the organization.

Greenpeace has not become more democratic over the years. Although it could not longer be described as an unstructured group, its internal democracy has not improved. It is easy to become a member: one only needs to donate money at the door. But the vast majority of members have no way to influence decisions and policy. This lack of internal democracy is noted by William K. Carroll and R. S. Ratner in an article on new social movements:

> Greenpeace has never aspired to a mass membership. Actually it has no formal membership; instead campaigners and office staff are paid employees, although their work is supplemented by that of volunteers. Volunteers and Greenpeace supporters – those who give money when contacted by the extensive canvass – have no rights to participate in decision making; they may define themselves as members but they are actually positioned as subscribers to the organization's glossy magazine.[17]

The positioning of members as subscribers with no decision making power prevents members from influencing the organization.[18] For example, even if someone wanted to change the orientation of Greenpeace by organizing a mass sign up of working class "members," they could do little to affect the organization internally.

This lack of internal democracy extends to the finances of Greenpeace. The budget and allocation of financial resources is decided by the Board of Directors of Greenpeace Canada. Members, or more accurately subscribers, have no input on the allocation of financial resources within Greenpeace. This issue came to the fore in 1993 when an internal memo was leaked revealing that only 5 per cent of the annual Greenpeace budget was

---

[17] William K. Carroll and R. S. Ratner, "Media Strategies and Political Projects: A Comparative Study of Social Movements," *Canadian Journal of Sociology* 24 (1999). 5.

[18] The membership numbers of Greenpeace are not published in their annual reports though some figures do exist. In their book on the history of Greenpeace Mark Warford and Kieran Mulvaney state that Greenpeace International had one 1 million members in 1985 and 4.8 million in 1990. Mark Warford, ed. *Greenpeace: Witness: Twenty-Five Years on the Environmental Front Line* (London: Andre Deutsh, 1996) It is estimated that Greenpeace Canada had 300,000 members in 1991 and less than half that in 1997. Ian Mulgrew, "Greenpeace Canada Fights Serious Financial Trouble," *Vancouver Sun* 8 September 1997.

dedicated to campaigns.[19] The annual budget of Greenpeace lists the total spent on different campaigns; however, this includes all the "administrative overhead" such as salaries, copying, postage, telephone, and a percentage of rent for space, which serves to inflate the amount spent on campaigns. A snapshot of how much money Greenpeace has had over the years is available by looking through their reports. In 1979 Greenpeace Canada had $158,571; in 1980 this increased to $390,339. Revenue in the late 1980s saw a dramatic increase: in 1987 it was $1,641,565 and in 1988 $2,977,092. The 1990s again saw major increase in revenue: in 1993 $7,543,402, in 1994 $6,749,521, in 1995 $5,571,486, and in 1996 $5,928,470.[20] Greenpeace is a comparatively wealthy organization in the world of social movements; however, its spending decisions lack even the basics of democracy.

The fact that Greenpeace lacks internal democracy may seem to be of concern only to the members. However, Greenpeace leaders have insisted that they are interested in expanding the scope of democracy and in speaking for a 'universal' humanity. It is this contradiction that needs to be highlighted. Greenpeace asserts that their struggle is against undemocratic corporations, a David vs. Goliath scenario with Greenpeace representing the people against the multi-national polluting corporations. Greenpeace has stated this explicitly. "The battle ground is the bitterly cold ice fields of the Labrador Front. Greenpeace Shepherds against industrial Goliaths" one account put it.[21] This claim to universality is restated in a variety of ways. Another Greenpeace writer put it this way: "Greenpeacers see themselves as a prototype United Nations peace force."[22] When Greenpeace was initiating its second anti-whaling campaign in 1976, it sought the endorsement of the United Nations and even had the UN extend the Vancouver Habitat conference so the launching of the *Greenpeace VII* from the Jericho Beach conference site would end the conference.[23] Robert Hunter goes as far as to say, "We were sailing out this time with the official endorsement of the United Nations conference – we *were* the world community."[24]

---

[19]   See "Greenpeace Canada at war with itself" *Ottawa Citizen* 9 June 1993, Canadian Press, "Greenpeace accused of betraying supporters: staff revolt rocks group" *Winnipeg Free Press* 10 June 1993 A3.

[20]   Greenpeace Canada, *Financial Statements* (Toronto: Greenpeace Canada, 1979 -96).

[21]   *Greenpeace Chronicles* 4 (Spring 1977), 1.

[22]   *Greenpeace Chronicles, 1: 1* (Autumn 1975), 1.

[23]   *Vancouver Sun* "Sending off Greenpeace Crews" 14 June 1976, 69.

[24]   Hunter, *Warriors,* 305. Emphasis in the original.

These claims fall apart under closer scrutiny. Greenpeace's actions to save the environment are not inherently beneficial to all. Despite their claims to be democratic, universal, and above class interests, the methods they choose often have very real negative effects on one particular group: the working-class. This was especially clear in one of its first Canadian campaigns. The campaign to ban the seal hunt devastated two entire economies and communities: the Inuit and the Newfoundland sealers. Though the stated intent of Greenpeace was to stop the large scale commercial sealers that were depleting the seals, this was not the end result. Greenpeace's narrow agenda to stop seal hunting was carried out at the expense of the working class and poor in the communities they were targeting.

CHAPTER THREE

SEALS, SENATORS, AND MOVIE STARS

The seal hunt has always been integral to the livelihood of both the Inuit and Newfoundlanders. Native peoples have relied on seals for oil, meat and clothing for thousands of years. From the migratory fishery of the sixteenth century to the later European settlements on Newfoundland in the seventeenth and early eighteenth century, sealing has played a major role in the economy and seal oil was a major export to Britain for use as lamp fuel.[1] Through the nineteenth century, as alternative fuel sources such as oil and gas were developed, the seal oil market declined, while the seal skin market increased.[2] The importance of sealing cannot be underestimated. In the middle of the nineteenth century goods produced through sealing accounted for over thirty per cent of Newfoundland's exports.[3] Ryan states, "the seal fishery had made an unparalleled contribution to Newfoundland and nothing – including agriculture, mining, paper milling, railroads, or free trade with the United States – could take its place."[4] The importance of the seal hunt to Newfoundlanders was not only economic. It created a whole culture, and working class solidarity among the sealing community. As historian Shannon Ryan notes, "the seal fishery …had a comprehensive influence on society and culture in general and contributed to the development, by 1914, of a distinctive Newfoundland identity."[5]

The hunt moved from an inland hunt to a sea-going hunt in small boats, and as industrialization increased the technology of getting out onto

---

[1] Shannon Ryan, *The Ice Hunters: A History of Newfoundland Sealing to 1914* (St. John's, Nfld.: Breakwater, 1994), 78

[2] Ryan, *The Ice Hunters*, 85.

[3] Guy David Wright, *Sons and Seals: A Voyage to the Ice* (St. John's, Nfld.: Institute of Social and Economic Research Memorial University of Newfoundland, 1984), 10.

[4] Ryan, *The Ice Hunters*, 117.

[5] Ryan, *The Ice Hunters*, 328.

the ice to conduct the seal hunt changed. [6] Small rowing boats gave way to the sailing era and the large vessel hunt, signaled by two schooners leaving St. John's in 1793. The steam era of 1863-1945 saw the sail schooners replaced by steam ships.[7] However, it must be noted that these technological changes did not result in an elimination of the earlier methods of sealing, as the large commercial sealers, the landsmen hunt, small ships, and individual sealers walking out to the ice, all coexisted together. It was the continued presence of the local landsman and small ship hunt that allowed Greenpeace to initially forge an alliance with the Newfoundland sealers against the large factory ships as the locals found the large hauls of the sealing ships a threat to their hunt.

The development of sealers was different from the more typical development of waged workers in Canada, however, this does not mean that there was no class struggle. The persistence of a truck system through most of the 19th century and the early 20th century created a set of different class relations. Sean Cadigan notes, "Truck represented a mutual, though unequal, accommodation between two basic classes: merchants and fish producers. Fish producers and merchants, like suppliers of labour and capital in other staple industries, needed each other, but this interdependency did not preclude struggle between the two."[8] He argues, "While the discourse of law may have fixed broad parameters, a very material class struggle governed the day-to day lives of residents of the northeast coast."[9] With the understanding that the truck system differed from direct waged labour it can be said that the sealers were the first members of the working-class in Newfoundland to take collective action, with a strike in 1832.[10] The striking sealers, fighting to get their wages

---

[6] Inland hunting and sealing from small boats did not stop. "The practice known as landsmen sealing, continues today; some landsmen simply walk onto the ice from their homes—and shoot adult seals. There are about 4,000 landsmen sealers in eastern Canada today. The pelts are sold and the meat is often eaten by the fishermen and their family." Wright, *Sons and Seals*, 10.

[7] Wright, Sons and Seals, 8-18 and Ryan, *The Ice Hunters*, 138-203.

[8] Sean T. Cadigan, *Hope and Deception in Conception Bay: Merchant-Settler Relations in Newfoundland, 1785-1855.* (Toronto: University of Toronto Press, 1995). P.101 It should also be noted that while Cadigan's book is primarily about the cod fishery he notes, and it is generally understood, that "Sealers were fisherman who simply engaged in a different industry for a short period of time each year. Merchants tried to use truck in the seal fishery just as they did in the cod fishery." p.102

[9] Cadigan, *Hope and Deception* p.100

[10] Ryan, *The Ice Hunters*,.329-330.

from the masters and merchants in cash, banded together. In the end, the strike was successful and the sealers demands were met. The feeling of solidarity was likely reinforced by the shared, class experience of suffering through terrible employment conditions, over-crowded ships, inadequate food, and exploitative pay arrangements that continued after the 1832 strike.[11]

A decline in the industry in the last half of the nineteenth century saw labour peace due more to sagging industry than better working conditions.[12] The last major strike was in 1902, again over working conditions, the cut given to the owners, and extra fees.[13] Like many of the feats, struggles, and heartaches of the sealer and the sealing community, the 1902 strike was commemorated in the song "The Sealers' Strike of 1902:"

Attention, all ye fishermen, and read this ballad down,
And hear about the sealers strike the other day in town;
When full three thousand northern men did walk the streets all day,
With cool determined faces they struck out to get fair play.

Each steamer's crew did fall in line, while cheers out loudly rang,
Led on by one brave Calloway, the hero of the gang.
Free berths it was their motto, and no man would give in,
A fight for death or glory, boys, this victory to win.

They halted just before the bank, when all hands fell in line;
They went inside to state their case before A.B. Morine.
He got the terms to suit the men, and from the van did call;
That he secured three fifty and "free berths" for one and all.

A ringing cheer the sealers gave, with hearts both light and gay.
And three more cheers they gave Morine, the man who won the day.
With happy hearts they fisted bags, as lightly they did trip,
With boots and bags and baking pan to get on board their ship.

Then soon around the northern head they disappeared from view,
Manned by a plucky, hardy race, a bully northern crew.
May they return with bumper trips, it is our earnest prayer
The boys who nobly showed their pluck, and fought to get their share.[14]

---

[11] For more on conditions see: Wright, *Sons and Seals*, 15.
[12] Ryan, *The Ice Hunters*, 342.
[13] Ryan, *The Ice Hunters*, 342-347.
[14] Shannon Ryan and Larry Small, *Haulin' Rope and Gaff: Songs and Poetry in the History of the Newfoundland Seal Fishery*, (St John's, Nfld.: Breakwater Books, 1978), 64.

The solidarity and the cultural remembrances of the strength of collective action of the sealers would be a reoccurring theme in response to the protests against the hunt.

Sealing slowed during World War One and stopped altogether during World War Two as steamers were brought into the war effort.[15] However the post-war period saw a rise in sealing, "as early as 1949 the combined catch of the Canadian and Norwegian fleets was double prewar levels."[16] It was in this period of the 1950s and 1960s that conservation became an issue and public protest began against the hunt. From this point forward there would be little agreement between the sealing and anti-sealing forces. The pivotal moment for the start of public support for protest against the hunt came when the French language CBC broadcast a film in 1964 on the seal hunt entitled *Les Phoques de la Barquise*. This film sensationalized the seal hunt by focusing on the brutality of the hunt, in particular the skinning of live seals. The negative impact of this film was immense and the live skinning of seals would become a predominant theme in the coming decades of protest.[17] It was later revealed that the live seal skinning footage had been faked. A fisher from Magdalen Island stated that he was paid to skin a live seal for the camera and that it was before sealing season had actually opened for the year."[18] Those protesting the seal hunt omitted this knowledge from the public and instead concentrated on the brutality of the hunt. Peter Lust, an avid anti-sealing voice, denies that the footage was faked in his book *The Last Seal Pup*. Lust also believed the harp seal was near extinction. His main source for information was Brian Davies, who would also become a famous protester. This extinction myth was repeated often by those in Greenpeace and became a reoccurring theme in the anti-sealing protest movement. In 1978 Greenpeace member Dan MacDermott stated in an interview:

> We maintain that wiping out a species, such as the harp seal, is an extreme circumstance which calls for extreme measures to make sure that stops.

---

[15] Wright, *Sons and Seals*; and James E. Candow, *Of Men and Seals: A History of the Newfoundland Seal Hunt* (Ottawa: Ministry of the Environment, 1989).

[16] Candow, *Of Men and Seals*, 113

[17] On the impact of this film see Candow, *Of Men and Seals*, 117; Wright, *Sons and Seals*, 22; and Janice Scott Henke, *Seal Wars: An American Viewpoint* (St. John's, Nfld.: Breakwater, 1985), 68-17. See Cynthia Lamson, *Bloody Decks and a Bumper Crop: The Rhetoric of Sealing Counter-Protest* (St. John's, Nfld.: Institute of Social and Economic Research, Memorial University of Newfoundland, 1979) for an examination of the rhetoric surrounding the seal protests.

[18] Candow, *Of Men and Seals*, 117; also see Wright, *Sons and Seals*, 22, for a similar account.

Many prominent scientists feel that it is ecologically insane to commercially exploit a species that is below its maximum sustainable yield.[19]

In fact, the concern for the harp seals was overstated, as there is little credible scientific basis for this extinction myth. As Cynthia Lomson points out in her book on the rhetoric of the protest:

> Interestingly, the harp seal does not appear on any official endangered species list, and, according to Fisheries Department biologist, Mac Mercer, the harp is the second most populous species of the planet's thirty-two types of seal. Even Dr. David Lavigne [a prominent anti-sealer] denied the alarmist position taken by the protesters.[20]

By instigating these protests, Greenpeace was taking an extreme stand, based on inaccurate or misleading information that set the organization against whole communities.

In 1976, when the first Greenpeace anti-sealing campaign was started, the organizers attempted to make in-roads within the Newfoundland sealing community and rally them against the big sealers. Greenpeace member Carl Rising-Moore had met members of the Newfoundland Fishermen, Food and Allied Workers Union (NFFAWU) in a pub in Cornerbrook, Newfoundland.[21] He convinced the president of NFFAWU, Richard Cashin, and members of the executive of the union to travel to St. Anthony's, the staging area for Greenpeace's forays onto the ice, to meet with representatives from Greenpeace. The talks to have Greenpeace and the Fisherman's union co-operate against the large foreign commercial sealing operations reached the point of a joint statement being issued by the two organizations. This statement advised that both would participate in a joint blockade of the ports of St. John's and Vancouver, closing them to all foreign trawlers and draggers by 1 June 1976, if the federal government did not declare a 200 mile fishing management zone around Canadian waters.[22] This was the strategy of Greenpeace, according to Robert Hunter, who was president of the Greenpeace foundation at the time. Hunter states that by the time the direct action campaign on the ice was at a close for the season, "We formed an alliance to go after the large icebreakers mainly from Norway, that were going into the birthing

---

[19] Lamson, *Bloody Decks*, 15.
[20] Lamson, *Bloody Decks,* 15.
[21] Hunter, *Warriors*, 270.
[22] Hunter, *Warriors,* 271.

grounds. These were the real threat to the continued viability of the seal herds." [23]

In their newspaper *Greenpeace Chronicles,* Greenpeace member Paul Watson explained why the anti-seal campaign accepted the alliance with the Newfoundland sealers:

> The fact is that the commercial fleets owned by Norwegian companies are wiping out the seal herds. The fact is the Norwegians destroyed three great herds of seals prior to starting on the Labrador herds in 1947. The fact is that the commercial fleets take only the pelts, leaving the meat on the ice, while the fishermen and Eskimo of Newfoundland and Labrador do eat the meat. With a conservation stand the seals could have a chance. [24]

However, Greenpeace would not follow through on this historic agreement and a year later in 1977, Paul Watson would contradict himself, insisting:

> The entire hunt must be stopped immediately and totally by both commercial and landsmen interests…the Greenpeace position is that we are totally opposed to the killing of all seals by Canadians, Norwegians, Danes, and others. [25]

Watson assumed control of the anti-sealing campaign in 1978 and left no room for confusion on his opinion towards sealers. In a CBC interview Watson stated:

> I certainly wasn't for striking any bargains with Newfoundland sealers. To me sealing is despicable and it has no economic foundation for even existing. It is a glorified welfare system. You know the government spends more money on it than it brings in. [26]

Greenpeace's position against all sealing meant that the opportunity for the more reasonable and mutually beneficial route of stopping the foreign corporate harvest and maintaining the low-scale, self-sufficient local harvest had been lost. It had been lost not just by a tactical mistake, but also by counterposing Greenpeace's environmentalist perspective against a working-class community's economic interests. It is not entirely clear what compelled

---

[23] "Greenpeace and the politics of image" *Ideas* CBC Radio Transcripts (Nov 9 and 16, 1993), 14.

[24] Paul Watson, "Shepards of the Labrador Front," *Greenpeace Chronicles* 2: 2 (1976), 6.

[25] *Greenpeace Chronicles,* 2: 3 (1976/77), 3.

[26] "Greenpeace and the politics of image" *Ideas* CBC Radio Transcripts (Nov 9 and 16, 1993), 14.

this abrupt change. According to Patrick Moore, a co-director of the anti-seal campaign, the reaction of the Greenpeace membership to the alliance with the NFFAWU was a factor:

> Last year we came in here determined to put an end to the commercial hunt only...As far as Newfoundland landsmen were concerned, guys who kill a few seals working out of small boats, we backed them all the way. Know what we got for our trouble? Stacks of Greenpeace membership cards, torn in half, pouring into the office in Vancouver.[27]

Moore's claim may be an exaggeration as the membership numbers in 1976 were low, with one estimate being 30 core members.[28] Watson states that there were a handful of buttons sent crushed up in a paper bag, hardly the stacks that Moore claims.[29] As well, the quotes from Watson in 1977 and 1978 show the Greenpeace leadership of the sealing campaign broke the alliance based as much on their own views as any other reason. Watson's own book that covers the events suggests that the alliance was struck only as a way out of a difficult situation when the Greenpeace team was met with such hostility in the first year of the campaign. After public support increased and became international, the alliance was no longer useful.[30]

Further evidence of how Greenpeace failed to rise above their professional managerial class bias is the way in which Greenpeace portrayed the seal hunt and the sealers. Greenpeace began to vilify the sealers, referring to the hunt as an "annual outrage"[31] and writing descriptive prose designed to sway the reader to share the outrage. A special edition of the *Greenpeace Chronicles* in 1977 was typical:

> Millions of baby seals began to come under the fatal shadow of the sealers and the sealers and their two week old lives were snuffed out by the cruel clubs and gaffs...They butchered every seal within sight, sparing none. Each and every year the sealers came, to stain the whitish blue floes scarlet

---

[27] Sandra Gwyn "The Media go to the Seal Hunt: Radical Chic versus the Newfie Swilers" *Saturday Night* (May 1977), 28.

[28] Brown and May, *The Greenpeace Story*, 40

[29] Paul Watson as told to Warren Rogers, *Sea Shepard: My Fight for Whales and Seals* (New York: W.W. Norton & Company, 1982) 88.

[30] Paul Watson, *Sea Shepard* (New York: W.W. Norton & Company, 1982) 87.

[31] Paul Watson, "Spring 77 Seal Campaign" *Greenpeace Chronicles* 2: 3 (76/77).

with the life-blood of the seals.[32]

Greenpeace did not stop at graphically and negatively portraying the seal hunt. It also mocked Newfoundland culture. One quote indicates the tone of its campaign. "It was called 'The Great Hunt' and the sealers were considered to be strong and courageous heroes. It always has been and still remains a brutal annual outrage of destruction."[33] Greenpeace attacked the sealers' pride in their work and cultural history as well as ridiculing entire Newfoundland communities.

The above is only a sampling of the rhetorical devices used in the campaign. The images of the seal hunt are vivid, such as the contrast of the seals' blood on the ice, and constructed to be extremely disturbing. It was easy to record the hunt, as it occurred outside, in public view, and Greenpeace emphasized that the harp seals were often killed at ten days old to increase public outrage towards the hunt and the sealers. The effect of the anti-seal campaign became evident with the incredible back-lash against the sealers. Thousands of letters were sent to government officials, newspapers, magazines, radio call-in shows, and to St. Anthony's, Newfoundland, addressed to sealers in general. A sampling of the letters illustrates how the anti-seal campaign had been received at home and abroad:

Sirs:
You people of Newfoundland are a bunch of murderers. You must love killing defenceless, baby seals. You feel that killing them is added income. With that money I hope you rot. I guess it's true, Newfoundland IS backward, ignorant and prehistoric.
D.B
Millwaukee, U.S.A.

Sealers
St. Anthony, Newfoundland

The pitiful sight of the mother seal looking at her skinned baby made my heart sick. If that is the only way these men can make a living, I hope they all starve to death. Better still, maybe we could CLUB them to death.
T.B.
Ontario, Canada[34]

---

[32] "Why We Do What We Do" *Greenpeace Chronicles "Special Edition"* 2: 4 (1977), 3.
[33] *Greenpeace Chronicles "Special Edition"* 2: 4 (1977), 3.
[34] These letters are from Henke, *Seal Wars,* 175-183 and the book contains many similar letters. Also see Francis Patey, *A Battle Lost: An Unsuccessful Attempt to*

This is only a sampling of thousands of letters. Author and anthropologist Janice Scott Henke has commented on the anti-seal campaign, noting that, "The tendency of the cultural anthropologist would be to view the protest movement as entirely unethical due to this blatant disregard for human impact, and its explicit denial of the intrinsic worth of Atlantic culture."[35] The enormous attention Greenpeace brought to bear on the sealers was overwhelming, and by attracting political and star power to the ice floes, Greenpeace maximized the number of people who would see the hunt and the sealers as negatively as possible.

After Greenpeace had dropped their alliance with the Newfoundland sealers, they recruited U.S. senate representatives to come North to condemn the hunt. The U.S. House of Representatives passed a motion condemning the hunt and Congressman Jeffords, a Republican, and Congressman Ryan, a Democrat, came to witness the hunt first-hand. Greenpeace activist Robert Hunter describes this as an attempt to "bring our new American political muscle to bear."[36] It seems Hunter missed the irony of using American imperialist pressure against the working class of his own country – the same imperialist power he had opposed in Greenpeace's first action against American nuclear tests. In addition to congressmen, Greenpeace solicited the help of movie stars; Henry Fonda and Gregory Peck went on the record condemning the seal hunt and Brigitte Bardot helicoptered in for photo ops on the ice flows.[37] Brigitte Bardot wrote a journal of her protest trip to the Newfoundland ice that was published in the *Greenpeace Chronicles.* Bardot participated in vilifying the sealers. "You are called Canadian Assassins. The word is out," she stated at a press conference.[38] In contrast, she likened the Greenpeace protesters to the apostles and admired their courage and devotion.[39] Greenpeace had traded in its alliance with workers for an alliance with senators and movie stars. Francis Patey, a sealer from a sealing family who wrote a first person account of the protests around St. Anthony's in the 1970s, writes one of the best summaries of how this campaign affected sealers. Patey writes,

---

Save the Seal Hunt (Grand Falls Nfld.: Robinson-Blackmore Printing and Publishing, 1990).

[35] Henke, *Seal Wars,* 110-111.

[36] Hunter, *Warriors,* 439.

[37] Gwyn "The Media"; Bob Wakeman, "Those Damned Seals Again" *Macleans* (January 1978), 21; and Ronald Bryden "They Impale Bleeding Hearts Don't They?" *Macleans* (March 20-27 1978).

[38] Brigitte Bardot, "A Labrador Journal," *Greenpeace Chronicles* 7 (June 1978).

[39] Bardot, "A Labrador Journal," *Greenpeace Chronicles* 7 (June 1978).

> We have read and listened for years now to the hate, the propaganda, the prejudice, the falsehoods, and the malice which has been dumped on Newfoundland and Labrador. However, in the interest of our own self-esteem, in the interest of truth and justice, we must always remember from whence [sic] the criticism comes. Primarily, it has come from people who have much to gain by seeking headlines, and by capturing close-ups before the cameras.[40]

In terms of media relations, the sealers had been outdone. Greenpeace enjoyed an almost complete victory in its campaign to ban the hunt. The European Economic Community announced a voluntary boycott on seal products in 1982. In 1983, this ban became mandatory. In 1985, a Royal Commission on Seals and the Sealing Industry in Canada was formed. The report from the commission was tabled 17 December 1986 and recommended a ban on hunting seal pups. The sealing by large off-shore vessels was banned in 1987; combined with the boycott of furs and seal products in Europe, all that remained was a much decreased landsmen hunt. The landsmen had started a co-operative in 1986, the Northeast Coast Sealers Co-operative, hoping to use seal pelts in Newfoundland crafts and restart the seal meat processing.[41] By 1990 the landsmen hunt still existed marginally and the co-op was still operating with the assistance of the Newfoundland government.[42]

The anti-sealing campaign was a success from Greenpeace's perspective, but it failed to take responsibility for destroying the economic and social basis of the Newfoundland sealing and Inuit communities. John Amagualik, an Inuit leader, states very succinctly what the Greenpeace campaigns against sealing meant:

> The collapse of the seal skin market meant that many of our communities could no longer depend on that income, and it resulted in an increase in the social problems that we have. When a person has nothing to do, sitting at home, he or she is more liable to get into alcohol and drug abuse. There was a marked increase in the rate of suicide among young people, especially in communities that depended heavily on the sealskin industry. So there was a devastating effect.[43]

---

[40] Patey, *A Battle Lost,* 80.
[41] See Candow, *Of Man and Seals,* 187-190 for the details on the post Royal Commission hunt.
[42] Patey, *A Battle Lost,* 82.
[43] "Greenpeace and the politics of image," *Ideas,* 11-12.

Clearly the impact was not solely economic and it affected the Inuit community. Amagualik testified to the Royal Commission on sealing about the cultural impact of the ban and boycotts noting that, "It is through the hunting of seals, and their butchering and distribution, that young people can readily be taught the virtues of cooperation, patience, sharing and their responsibilities in the community."[44]

The economic devastation was also attested to by Newfoundland sealers plight. In 1978 the average Newfoundland sealer earned less than $8,000 per year from all sources and it was predicted that a ban on seal hunting would reduce the average sealers income by 15 to 30 per cent and would take $5.5 million dollars out of the Newfoundland economy.[45] In 1985 the testimony of a sealer brings the impact of a ban into perspective,

> We survive month to month, year to year, living in hope for better times. On average, our incomes are well below the poverty line, yet we live a lifestyle that brings great day-to-day satisfaction. We have often heard from our critics that men such as myself only earn a few hundred dollars a year from sealing. Therefore, it is of no great economic benefit. But Canadians and this Royal Commission must realize that for families living near the poverty line, a few hundred dollars means a lot. Without that money we can't continue to make money, because we need it to reinvest in the rest of the year's fishery.[46]

Ironically, the hunt ban resulted in an annual culling of seals anyway. "If the hunt were banned," warned Mac Mercer, a marine biologist from McGill and Harvard, "we'd have to go quietly and bop off an annual quota of seals anyway, just to protect the fishery."[47] This is what has happened. The ship-based hunt has been eliminated and the landsmen hunt continued in limited form with an annual quota of seals throughout the 1990s.

The battle over the seal hunt reappeared off the North Eastern Coasts of Canada in the first decade of the 21st century with Greenpeace once again active in trying to ban the seal hunt in its entirety. Greenpeace published a report, *Canadian Seal Hunt: No Management and No Plan* in response to a large increase in the total allowable catch (TAC) of harp seals in Newfoundland Labrador. The Greenpeace report was concerned with the implementation of the Canadian governments Atlantic Seal Hunt Management plan that set the total allowable catch for harp seals at the

---

[44] Testimony from the Royal Commission on Sealing as reprinted in Henke, *Seal Wars*, 203.
[45] Bryden "They Impale Bleeding Hearts Don't They?"
[46] Henke, *Seal Wars*, 200.
[47] Gwyn "The Media go to the Seal Hunt," 27.

highest level since 1971 when a cap on allowable catch was first introduced. Greenpeace, it appeared at first glance, was concerned with the higher levels of seals allowed to be taken under the new management plan. However, it quickly becomes clear that they are still advocating for an all out ban.

> Continuation of the Canadian commercial hunt cannot be viewed as consistent with maintenance of the long-term conservation status of the harp seal, which is likely to be increasingly threatened by the onset of climate change-related impacts to the sea ice ecosystem. Until such time as the substantial uncertainties surrounding the status of, and various pressures on harp seal populations can be fully resolved, including those relating to climate change, such that reliable assessment and control could feasibly be exercised, the only sustainable and scientifically justifiable course of action must be to suspend the commercial hunt immediately. In fact, it is virtually certain that most of these uncertainties will never be adequately resolved.[48]

The current TACs may be unsustainable. There are legitimate concerns attached to the sustainability of sealing activities, and to the lack of a precautionary ethic driving the current management paradigms. However, the previously cited Greenpeace report makes it clear that Greenpeace wants to ban all commercial sealing. In addition, the conditions Greenpeace set to resume the hunt will, by their own admission, likely never be met. So they are playing a bit of a shell game. Suggesting on the one hand that a better estimation system for TAC and a precautionary ethic would alleviate their concerns and then stating that there will never be an adequate resolution to their concerns. To their credit the Greenpeace report acknowledges that they do not oppose an aboriginal hunt, there is an explanatory note that states "Greenpeace does not oppose the indigenous hunt in Canada and Greenland."[49] It stands to reason that they may have also reversed their position on the traditional Newfoundlander landsmen hunt. However, this is not the case. This call for a complete ban on the hunt was being put forward by Greenpeace in a time that they note

---

[48] Paul Johnston and David Santillo, *The Canadian Seal Hunt: No Management, No Plan* (The Netherlands: PrimaveraQuint Greenpeace International, March 2005), 3

[49] Paul Johnston and David Santillo, *The Canadian Seal Hunt: No Management, No Plan* (The Netherlands: PrimaveraQuint Greenpeace International, March 2005), 3

themselves, "the harp seal is currently the most abundant seal species on the Canadian ice"[50]

It is clear that the seal hunt is still an important part of the rural Newfoundlanders livelihood. Yet the same people who dismissed these claims in the 1970s and '80s continue to do so in the 21st century. The same people are making very similar attacks on the working people of Newfoundland and Labrador. Paul Watson stated in the 1970s that, "sealing is despicable and it has no economic foundation for even existing."[51] To his credit he remains consistent stating in 2005 that, "It's a barbaric and ignorant and cruel industry. And it can't be justified just because somebody's making a buck off of it."[52] The hunt continues to be portrayed as one conducted by outside interests with the significance of the seal hunt to Newfoundlanders being framed as insignificant. The DFO responds to these criticisms stating;

> Estimates from DFO and the province of Newfoundland and Labrador find that between 5,000 and 6,000 individuals derive some income from sealing. This is approximately 1 per cent of the total provincial population, and 2 per cent of the labour force. This is a substantial number of individuals in the context of small rural communities. Many other locally-important industries share this characteristic. For example, crop production and forestry each account for less than 1 per cent of Canadian GDP, but their local economic importance is undisputable.[53]

Much like the continued dismissal of rural Newfoundlanders reliance on the hunt the idea that seals are skinned alive has also persisted. The International Fund for Animal Welfare (IFAW) claims that, "If you were to witness this cruelty personally, your heart would break. Newborn seals skinned or bled alive ... clubbed to death ... or shot and left wounded to die under the ice."[54] They continue to put forward this claim even after the

---

[50] Paul Johnston and David Santillo, *The Canadian Seal Hunt: No Management, No Plan* (The Netherlands: PrimaveraQuint Greenpeace International, March 2005), 3

[51] "Greenpeace and the politics of image" *Ideas* CBC Radio Transcripts (Nov 9 and 16, 1993), 14.

[52] CBC News "'MacGyver' tackles seal hunt" Tuesday, March 8, 2005 Accessed January 14, 2011

[53] Department of Fisheries and Oceans Canada, "Frequently Asked Questions About Canada's Seal Harvest" DFO website http://www.dfo-mpo.gc.ca/fm-gp/seal-phoque/faq-eng.htm#_19 Accessed January 14, 2011

[54] IFAW, "Save Baby Seals, End the Seal Hunt" IFAW website http://www.ifaw.org/ifaw_european_union/join_campaigns/save_baby_seals_end_the_seal_hunt/index.php

Canadian Veterinary Association Journal published a report that found, "the large majority of seals taken during this hunt (at best, 98% in work reported here) are killed in an acceptably humane manner. However, the small proportion of animals that are not killed effectively justifies continued attention to this hunt on the part of the veterinary profession."[55] The report addresses the IFAW claims very specifically but the IFAW disagrees with the way the report is discussed. The Department of Fisheries and Oceans cites the CVA report among others and states on their website that, "Seals are not skinned alive. Independent international veterinarians and European Food Safety Authority (EFSA) experts concluded that the suggestions by anti-sealing groups that many seals are skinned alive are not true."[56] The persistence of the seals skinned alive myth shows how powerful this image is. Newfoundland sealers are continually vilified by the environmental movement often using dubious evidence.

Environmental groups have even continued Greenpeace's tactic of recruiting movie and television stars to the ice floes. MacGyver, also known as Richard Dean Anderson, posed on the ice flows at the behest of Paul Watson and the Sea Shepherd Society.[57] Brigit Bardot made the visit again along with a long list of celebrities. Bardot, at the time in her 70s did not make it to the ice but she was in Ottawa denouncing the hunt. "You must join me to ensure this hunt stops," Bardot said in front of a fake picture showing a seal clubbing a human baby."[58] So many celebrities have spoken out against the hunt that it has become entertainment news. In 2006 the entertainment section of a CanWest news site noted,

> Pamela Anderson, Brigitte Bardot and Sir Paul McCartney have made headlines in recent weeks speaking out against Canada's seal hunt – but they are not the only celebrities who have been vocal with their

---

Accessed January 14, 2011

[55] Pierre-Yves Daoust, Alice Crook, Trent K. Bollinger, Keith G. Campbell, and James Wong, "Animal welfare and the harp seal hunt in Atlantic Canada" Can Vet J. 2002 September; 43(9): 687–694.

[56] Department of Fisheries and Oceans Canada, "Canadian Seal Harvest – Myths and Reality" DFO website http://www.dfo-mpo.gc.ca/fm-gp/seal-phoque/myth-eng.htm#_06 Accessed January 14, 2011

[57] CBC News "'MacGyver' tackles seal hunt" Tuesday, March 8, 2005 Accessed January 14, 2011

[58] CanWest News Service, "Stars and seals" April 7, 2006
http://www.canada.com/topics/entertainment/story.html?id=f52f3a77-129f-4dbf-82f0-af4bce5a1762&k=89397
Accessed January 14, 2011

complaints. Since the 1970s, a string of stars have tried to stop the annual cull by protesting one way or another the slaughter of seals, who are undeniably much more cute than pigs.[59]

The statement that baby seals are much cuter than pigs may seem oddly off topic but it is an important point. The Inuit sealers were not just affected by the harp seal hunt ban. While the Greenpeace campaign in the 1970s and '80s specifically targeted harp sealing, it also had an adverse effect on the ringed seal market, which was very important to the Inuit economy. Ringed seals are not cute and cuddly when young, and that is likely why they were not part of the campaign, although the ringed seal demand was equally decreased.[60] James E. Candow explores this idea in his history of the seal hunt, *Of Men and Seals.* Candow credits Pol Chantraine, a sealer and journalist, for the explanation of the subconscious appeal to the images of the harp seal pups.[61]

> Chantraine saw that a whitecoat shares many of the same characteristics that adults respond to in a child: proportionately large head, large low-lying eyes, and awkward movements. He concluded that the physical appearance of the whitecoat subconsciously triggers protective behaviour among humans.[62]

The rhetoric around the seal hunt has not changed. It still heavily relies on the reaction humans have to baby seals even though the hunt of baby seals has been outlawed. The website Harpseals.org which is "working to end the harp seal slaughter" prominently features pictures of baby harp seals and graphic pictures of whitecoats on the ice in pools of blood.[63] The same players are still involved. In Harpseals.org's section on the history of the hunt it has an essay by Paul Watson entitled "Seal Wars" in which he uses similar rhetoric that he used in the 1970s. He refers to "this lust to kill the seal" claiming "credible witnesses, including myself, have seen seals skinned alive and tortured."[64] Harpseals.org also has a section dedicated to sealers in which they display archival pictures of sealers with bloody whitecoats. The sites dedication is intended to be ironic:

---

[59] CanWest News Service, "Stars and seals" April 7, 2006
[60] George Wenzel, "The Harp-seal Controversy and the Inuit Economy" *Arctic,* 31: 1 (1978), 3-6.
[61] Candow, *Of Man and Seals,* 181.
[62] Candow, *Of Man and Seals,* 181.
[63] http://www.harpseals.org/index.php
[64] Paul Watson, "Seal Wars" 2003
http://www.harpseals.org/about_the_hunt/sealwars.php accessed January 22, 2011

Harpseals.org dedicates these photos of slaughtered whitecoat harp seals with the sealers to

1) all the seal hunt proponents who hate the fact that seal hunt opponents occasionally use images of white baby seals to stir emotion and energy against their cherished slaughter.

2) all the grey baby harp seals that the white baby harp seals turn into after molting at the ripe old age of 10-14 days, who have died at the hands of the killers.

NOTE: We acknowledge that the Canadian government now prohibits the killing of whitecoat harp seals, but allows the slaughter of hundreds of thousands of baby harp seals who have partially or completely molted their white coats. These baby seals are killed in the same exact manner: by beating them to death using clubs, sticks, and hakapiks or by shooting them in the head.[65]

I suppose I would be one of those who draw attention to the use of the images of baby white seals to stir up emotion, but anyone who visits the website of harpseals.org can determine for themselves that they do not occasionally use images of cute whitecoats: they use them repeatedly and base most of their campaign around the image. In fact harpseals.org has an online store in which you can purchase t-shirts, magnets, hand painted rocks, and canvases, all featuring the cute baby whitecoat harp seal, which it bears repeating can no longer be hunted under Canadian law.[66]

In the end, Greenpeace grew in membership and its media presence soared. There was little said about the communities left behind. Since the resumption of a larger hunt the same rhetorical devices are being used to vilify sealers and the traditional landsmen hunt. The Newfoundlanders have their own critique of Greenpeace that seems as timely today as it did when it was written, using a traditional cultural medium, a folk song, "Save Our Swilers:"

Come all you Newfoundlanders and listen to my song
About St. Anthony's visitors from "away" and "upalong";
There were movie types and media types and Mounties, some fivescore,
If we were bent on violence they'd need a hundred more.

---

[65] http://www.harpseals.org/about_the_hunt/sealergallery.php
[66] http://www.harpseals.org/e-store/index.php

They are out to ban the seal hunt and this they mean to do,
Brian Davis and the Greenpeacers and all their motley crew;
This year they've got Franz Weber with phony fur to sell—
A bleeding heart from Switzerland who thinks he's William Tell.

They say the seals are threatened but the evidence is clear,
With quotas carefully controlled, of that there is no fear;
We're the endangered species who live by coastal seas,
We kill the seal as we kill to feed our families.

A bedlamer boy from Greenpeace he chained on to the "whip,"
And was dunked into the water by the rolling of the ship;
We had a job to save him in all the fuss and racket,
But I bet his pelt wouldn't have been worth as much as a Ragged Jacket.

When Brigitte said in Paris she cuddled a whitecoat dear,
Sure every swiler in the land he grinned from ear to ear;
He knows from long experience she's pilin' on the lies,
A real whitecoat's talons would have slashed her face and eyes.

They call us cruel, barbaric, hunting seals just for the thrill
These pampered city slickers that a day's hard work would kill;
What do they know of challenges of storm and sea and ice
That dare the blood to answer and to pay the sealers' price?

They're out for front-page stories, they've come so far to roam,
And blood on ice will show up well on T. V. screens back home;
They know their media bosses have paid good money out,
If they don't send "juicy" stories their jobs are "up the spout."

There's many things we don't approve in countries far away
How people act and dress and talk and how they earn their pay;
But we don't get up a hate campaign and stir up children too,
To force our views on other folks as these do-gooders do.

Our government must keep these types from off the whelping ice,
Or there'll be tragedies to tell – we're men, not frightened mice;
We merit more protection than a motion on the floor
Where will you get your slippers when the seal hunt is no more?

We're not averse to meeting up with a star from Hollywood,
We sure would like to rescue her from an angry old Dog Hood;
But the Arctic floes are not the place, Yvette, to use your wiles,
We're not spruced up for courtin' when we're out there peltin' swiles!

We have to take from Nature whate'er the season bring,
We're fishermen in summer and swilers in the spring;
If you don't approve the seal hunt, you have a right to say,
But when we go out on that ice, don't try to bar our way.

So here's a health to Romeo, who took the sealer's part,
He stood up to protesters, he has our cause at heart;
And raise your glass to Tommy Hughes who tells it like he knows,
And don't forget Rich Cashin when you're culling friends from foes.[67]

For all its claims of representing the world community Greenpeace's anti-sealing campaign did not represent the working class communities of Newfoundland or Labrador. Through skilled use of media images and by mobilizing star power Greenpeace presented a one sided argument to the world community. In addition to a lack of consultation with the affected communities, Greenpeace's class bias was illustrated by initially brokering a deal with the working-class and then breaking it when it appeared the working-class was a liability not an asset. Although it is beyond the scope of this book to fully explore, the intersection of race and class as axes of oppression is suggested by the case of the Inuit in the sealing campaign. Though that seems to have been recognized by Greenpeace since its original campaign it raises more questions about Greenpeace's claim to universality. The disregard for working-class concerns and the local economies that Greenpeace illustrated in their anti-sealing campaign was repeated in BC when Greenpeace entered the debate around BC's ongoing struggle for a coherent sustainable forestry strategy.

---

[67] A. R. Scammell, "Save our Swilers," reprinted with permission from *Decks Awash* 6:4 (June 1977), 6, in Shannon Ryan and Larry Small, *Haulin' Rope and Gaff*, 156-7.

CHAPTER FOUR

GREENPEACE, LOGGERS, AND UNIONS

In July of 1997, Greenpeace found two of its ships, the *Arctic Sunrise* and the *Moby Dick,* blockaded into port in Vancouver by angry members of the Industrial Wood and Allied Workers of Canada.[1] The struggle between loggers and environmentalists is almost legendary in BC, yet beneath the headlines is a conflict that escapes easy analysis. The positioning of the argument as jobs versus the environment has been a successful tool used by timber companies and pro-business lobby groups to divide and conquer their critics but it is a false dichotomy. Unfortunately Greenpeace's strategy around forestry issues often exacerbates the conflict. On the other side, Share BC groups and the pro-business lobby group BC Forest Alliance have served to fan the flames against environmentalists encouraging workers that they are to blame for the problems of the industry.

The debate around forestry and conservation issues goes back to the turn of the century in British Colombia. From the early industrialists who considered themselves conservationists, such as H.R. MacMillian, to the scandals around tenure in the 1950s, the balance between corporate and community interests has been hotly debated. In 1905, BC premier Richard McBride opened up BC to corporate logging interests. McBride created special licences that would allow companies to log Crown land for a period of twenty-one years. Within three years there were 15,000 such licences granted.[2] With rapid advances in technology, the logging industry continued to grow. The introduction of steam power in the 1900s meant

---

[1] Paul Evans, "Greenpeace Ships Hemmed In" *The Province*, (3 July, 1997), A6; Glenn Bohn and Kim Pemberton, "IWA Demands $250,000 in lost wages to release Greenpeace ships" *The Vancouver Sun*, (4 July 1997), A4; Glenn Bohn, "Greenpeace considers options as move to free two ships fail" *The Vancouver Sun*, (5 July 1997), A7. It should be noted that the IWA was know as the International Woodworkers of America until the name change to Industrial Wood and Allied Workers of Canada in 1995.

[2] Ken Drushka, *Working in the Woods: A History of Logging on the West Coast*, (Madeira Park BC: Harbour Publishing, 1992), 59.

that despite a labour shortage during World War I, logging levels reached a record high.[3] By the 1930s, H.R. MacMillan, disturbed by the lack of any coherent forest conservation policy, issued a statement that sounds very much like a contemporary concern:

> "How long can it last?" it may be asked. "What of the future?" Canadians have listened to such tales of Canada's limitless resources that they are prone to avoid an answer rather than seek it. ...Meantime it is generally known among the well-informed that the forest is being overcut at a devastating rate in every forest province in Canada.[4]

The Sloan Commission was set up in 1945 to investigate the forest industry, and issued reports in both 1945 and 1957. Upon its recommendations, forest companies were granted long-term logging rights upon the condition that mills would be built and employment created for the communities.[5] Sustainable yield was the buzzword of the commission, though it meant little in terms of actual sustainability and more on how much companies were allowed to cut. Logging would expand greatly from the 1960s onwards introducing significant changes in technology.[6]

Contrary to popular rhetoric, loggers have long been interested in sane, environmentally sound practices in logging. As Jerry Lembcke and William M. Tattam point out in their book *One Union in Wood*, "Under Communist editorship the IWA's paper, the *Timberworker*, opposed clearcutting of forests and log exports and promoted reforestation and conservation."[7] The *Timberworker's* position makes sense, for workers stand to lose when technologies for faster, more profitable, and less environmentally sound logging are implemented and workers are eliminated. The IWA in the late 1940s correctly anticipated what lay ahead for its members. Labour saving technological advances would devastate

---

[3] Drushka, *Working in the Woods,* 77. See also Gordon Hak, *Turning Trees into Dollars: The British Columbia Coastal Lumber Industry 1858-1913* (Toronto: University of Toronto Press, 2000).

[4] Ken Drushka, *HR: A Biography of H.R. MacMillan* (Madeira Park BC: Harbour Publishing, 1995) 184.

[5] See Patricia Marchak, "Commentary" *BC Studies* 119 (1998), 73.

[6] For a fairly comprehensive history see Jeremy Wilson *Talk and Log: Wilderness Politics in British Columbia, 1965-96* (Vancouver: UBC Press, 1998); also see Ray Travers, "History of Logging and Sustained Yield in BC, 1911-90," *Forests Planning Canada*, 8: 1 (1992).

[7] Jerry Lembcke and William M. Tattam, *One Union in Wood: A Political History of the International Woodworkers of America* (BC: Harbour Publishing, 1984).

the workers in the forest industries and wreak even more havoc on the natural environment.[8]

The issue of technological change is a daunting one for all resource workers. Forestry workers have been particularly hard-hit over the past thirty years. Over the past three decades the annual volume of timber logged in BC has tripled while direct forestry jobs per thousand cubic metres have been cut in half.[9] Joyce Nelson identifies two key moments in forestry that resulted in huge job losses: 1974-1975 when the grapple yarder was introduced and 1983-1984 when giant faller bunchers were introduced.[10] Yarding refers to moving the cut trees from where they are cut to where they can be transported out of the cut block, either a road or landing. Highlead yarding was used up to the 1970s. This technique needed crews of five to six people; grapple yarders need only crews of two or three people.[11] The introduction of the feller buncher also had consequences for the workers. As Marchak points out, "Felling and bunching, for example, are now done by operators in mobile machines. One machine driver can log far more trees in a morning than the skilled faller of the past could have done in several days, and the driver never leaves his cab."[12]

The workers in the forestry industry have been devastated by the changes and it clearly is not because production slowed down. Since 1980 production has increased while employment has decreased in logging, sawmills and planing mills, and pulp and paper mills. By 1995 employment in logging had decreased by 23 per cent from 1980 and production had increased by 21 per cent. In sawmills and planing mills

---

[8] For a detailed history of all the technological changes in forestry see Ken Drushka and Hannu Konttinen, *Tracks in the Forest: The Evolution of Logging Machinery* (Helsinki, Finland: Timberjack Group Oy, 1997). See also Richard A. Rajala, *Clearcutting the Pacific Rain Forest: Production, Science, and Regulation* (Vancouver: UBC Press, 1998).

[9] Joyce Nelson, "Technology, Not Environmentalism Cuts Forest Jobs" *Witness to Wilderness: The Clayoquot Sound Anthology* Howard Breen-Needham et.al eds. (Vancouver: Arsenal Pulp Press,1994), 99.

[10] Nelson, "Technology, Not Environmentalism," 100.

[11] For a detailed explanation of the four major types of yarding – ground based, cable, balloon, and helicopter – see Scientific Panel for Sustainable Forest Practices in Clayoquot Sound, *Sustainable ecosystem Management in Clayoquot Sound: Planning and Practices* Report 5 (Victoria: Clayoquot Scientific Panel, 1995), 91-117.

[12] M. Patricia Marchak, Scott L. Aycock and Deborah M. Herbert *Falldown: Forest Policy in British Columbia* (Vancouver: David Suzuki Foundation and Ecotrust Canada,1999) 102.

employment had dropped by 18.8 per cent and production had increased by 18.7 per cent. Pulp and paper mills experienced similar trends: 18.8 per cent of the labour force had been cut and production had increased 22.7 per cent between 1980 and 1994.[13] It should be difficult to blame environmentalists for these types of numbers. However, blaming environmentalists allows the companies to play a game of bait and switch between workers and environmentalists. The companies say the environmentalists are to blame for the loss of jobs while the environmentalists incite the workers by blockading them from earning a living, leaving the companies relatively unscathed. This takes the focus off real issues such as overproduction, technological changes, and capitalist imperatives to increase production and profits and cut costs, such as labour.

Attempts had been made before to work out the issues between loggers and environmentalists without conflict. The Tin Wis Coalition was formed in 1988 with the intention of bringing workers, environmentalists, and First Nations together to talk about their interests. Recognizing the membership of the three groups were not mutually exclusive helped to bring the groups together. The models discussed and advocated in these forums were worker-oriented solutions, meaning solutions that were about employment, safety, and sustainability, not company profits. Solutions were largely based on the decentralization of forestry operations and community control over the means of production.[14] The source of the conflict was seen as an economic system that valued profit over workers and the environment. The Tin Wis participants committed themselves

> to develop and implement the mechanisms for Native people, trade unionists, environmentalists, women, youth and others to work together on a regional basis to resolve resource development and environmental issues and conflicts and to further the process of developing a "peoples" alternative to the policies of the present government.[15]

Unfortunately the coalition ceased activity shortly after its October 1990 conference in which they agreed to draft an alternate forest stewardship

---

[13] Marchak, Aycock and Herbert *Falldown,* 104-105. The raw employment data of Statistics Canada from which these statistics are derived is contained in Appendix C of *Falldown* 197-199.

[14] Evelyn W. Pinkerton, "Co-Management Efforts as Social Movements: The Tin Wis Coalition and the Drive for Forest Practices Legislation in BC" *Alternatives* 19(3), Tin Wis Coalition. Forest Stewardship Act, Draft Model Legislation of the Forestry Working Group, Vancouver, BC.

[15] *The New Catalyst,* 21.

act. The Tin Wis proposal would have been a radical departure from the mutual distrust entrenched on both the workers and environmentalist camps. Adopting such a way forward could have been the beginning of a counter hegemonic bloc that had class and race as an integral components in proposing a solution. Environmental writer Michael M'gonigle has expanded on these kind of solutions in the book *Forestopia*, a blueprint for value-added logging and a made in BC solution to the years of conflict between workers, environmentalists, and the industry. He does this by recognizing that the interests of workers is in sustainable forests, liveable communities, and control over the work process and their livelihoods. When solutions are framed with workers included, and indeed integral, to solving the problem of environmental degradation, then the confrontation between workers and environmentalists can be bridged.[16] However, workers have been largely excluded from decision-making in the conflict over forestry issues like Clayoquot Sound, and a coalition or people's alternative has remained elusive.

In 1989 the Social Credit government in BC formed an eleven member task force whose mandate was to find compromises for land use in Clayoquot Sound that satisfied all the stakeholders.[17] The task force was unable to reach an agreement, and by October 1989, it had been disbanded, with recommendations for a steering committee with more members and broader representation to take up the task. The next attempt was the Clayoquot Sound Development Steering Committee that had representatives from the logging industry, environmentalists, tourist operators, and First Nations.[18] Talks went on for over a year and a half until the environmental representatives walked out because logging continued while they met. The government had decided to have a separate panel composed of Ministry of Environment and Ministry of Forests representatives to decide where logging could occur, while the Steering Committee met. Failing to reach agreement on this, the environmentalists left the committee in May of 1991. The tourism representative left in

---

[16] Michael M'Gonigle and Ben Parfitt, *Forestopia: A Practical Guide to the New Forest Economy* (Madeira Park, BC: Harbour Publishing, 1994).

[17] The Clayoquot Sound Sustainable Development Task Force, *Report to the Minister of Environment and the Minister of Regional and Economic Development.* (Victoria: The Task Force,1991).

[18] More specifically there were representatives form the Nu-Chah-Nulth tribal Council, the City of Port Alberni, the District of Tofino, the Village of Ucluelet, the Regional District of Alberni-Clayoquot and representatives of aquaculture, environment, fishing, labour, mining, small business, large and small forest companies, tourism, six provincial ministries and two federal departments.

solidarity but was replaced by another tourism representative.[19] The
Steering Committee broke up with no formal agreement; however, when
the NDP formed government in 1991 they used the information and work
of both the Task Force and the Steering Committee in their land use plan
announced in 1993.[20] On 13 April 1993 the NDP government put forward
a land use plan for Clayoquot Sound that they hoped would end the
conflict over old growth, at least in that region.[21] Under the NDP's plan,
called the Clayoquot Sound land use decision, 44.7 per cent was
designated for commercial timber use under the label "general integrated
management." The plan also called for 33.4 per cent of the region to be
protected from logging in "protected areas," and 17.6 per cent was to be a
special management area broken into three categories: recreation, 1.1 per
cent; wildlife, 1.3 per cent; and scenic corridors, 15.2 per cent.[22]

The Friends of Clayoquot Sound, who had walked out of the Socred
talks, had put up blockades in 1992 but on a smaller scale than they would

---

[19] *Clayoquot Land Use Decision: Background Report* p.5. For an interesting
analysis of the actual consensus process itself see, Diane Leigh Marie Macqueen,
"Consensus Based Decision-making: The Clayoquot Sound Steering Committee
Process," MA thesis, Simon Fraser University, Burnaby, BC, 1996. Also, Craig
Darling, *In Search of Consensus: An Evaluation of the Clayoquot Sound
Sustainable Development Task Force Process,* (Victoria: University of Victoria
Institute for Dispute Resolution, 1991).

[20] For more detail about the rationale for the decisions in the land use plan see,
Province of British Columbia, *The Government of British Columbia Response to
the Commission on resources and Environment's Public Report and
Recommendations Regarding Issues Arising From the Clayoquot Land Use
Decision.* (Victoria, BC: Province of British Columbia, 1993); and for public
debate surrounding the decision see, Richard Watts, "Clayoquot group wants no-
logging area 2 1/2 times larger", *Victoria Times-Colonist* (28 August 1992), B16;
Peter W. Kennedy, "Cost analysis should decide Clayoquot fate" *Times-Colonist*
(1 November 1992); Cheri Burda, Fred Gale and Michael M'Gonigle, "Eco-
Forestry Versus the State(us) Quo: Or Why Innovative Forestry is Neither
Contemplated Nor Permitted Within the State Structure of British Columbia,"
Marchak, "Commentary," Michael Church, "Commentary"; Cheri Burda et.al,
"Reply," *BC Studies*, 119 (1998), 45-82.

[21] Office of the Premier, "Clayoquot Decision Balances Environmental, Economic
and Social values" News Release (Victoria, Province of BC, 13 April,1993).

[22] Province of British Columbia, *Clayoquot Sound Land Use Decision: Key
Elements* (Victoria: Province of British Columbia, April 1993). *Clayoquot Land
Use Decision: Background Report* (Victoria: Queen's Printer for British Columbia,
1993). The land protected within Clayoquot Sound went from 39,100 hectares to
87,600 hectares, increasing the percentage of protected land from 15 to 33 per cent.

in 1993. Over the summer and fall of 1993 the protests in the Sound would eventually attract more than 11,000 protesters.[23] In a series of confrontations over the summer of 1993, Greenpeace pursued a full preservationist agenda. Backing up the Friends of Clayoquot Sound and providing money, campaigners, and a formidable public relations machine, Greenpeace played a large part in bringing thousands of protesters into the Sound. Over 800 people were arrested, the largest number of persons ever arrested for social protest in Canada.

Some participants felt that making workers the target and not directly taking on the companies allowed the corporations to avoid scrutiny while furthering the split between workers and environmentalists. David Peerla, a Greenpeace forest campaigner at the time, was uncomfortable with the focus on workers and eventually left Greenpeace:

> I never wanted to put my campaign into direct conflict with labour, because I thought that was a false antagonism. So I never organized any direct civil disobedience which prevented workers from going to work in the forest…I was really confronting what I saw as the fundamental opponent: namely capital – the corporate sector.[24]

The complexities of a campaign that was meant to put pressure on forest companies but ended up in direct conflict with workers was never adequately addressed by Greenpeace. The companies were able to falsely, but persuasively, set the workers against the environmentalists claiming their jobs were at stake. This would not have been as easy had the environmentalists not been keeping them from work, however temporarily.

There is no simple solution to this bait and switch tactic yet communication would go a long way to usurping the companies tactic of playing on the mutual distrust between the two groups. In fairness, this cannot be laid completely at the door of the environmentalists; the mistrust was mutually reinforced. A source of the mistrust was the publicity efforts of the corporate lobby group the BC Forest Alliance and also Share BC

---

[23] For the previous years protests see Richard Watts, "List of protester-arrests grows at Clayoquot logging blockade" *Victoria Times-Colonist* (18 July 1992) A12; Richard Watts and Roger Stonebanks, "25 arrested as anti-logging protesters beef up Clayoquot battleline" *Times-Colonist* (1 August 1992) A3; Lynda Cassels, Clayoquot protesters stand firm" *Monday Magazine* (27 August 1992); Roger Stonebanks, "Clayoquot trials over as last of protesters given jail time, probation" *Times-Colonist,* (30 January 1993).

[24] "Greenpeace and the Politics of Image, *"Ideas,* 35.

groups.[25] Share groups follow the model of the Wise Use movement in the United States.[26] The Library of Parliament in Ottawa published a report entitled *Share Groups in B.C.* The paper delineates the links between the Share Movement, the timber industry and the Wise-Use movement. The conclusion of the paper argues that while, "grassroots movements and lobbying activity are legitimate and desirable in a democratic society, they are open to criticism if deliberately misrepresenting either the identity of interest involved or their goals".[27] The Wise Use movements' connections to both the American Freedom Coalition, which as the political arm of the Unification Church has supported right-wing regimes in Central and South America, and forestry corporations, makes its position as a grassroots roots movement dubious[28]. However, while recognizing industry backed protest for what it is, the complete dismissal of workers concerns would be a mistake. Many who joined Share groups would likely have been looking for an avenue to protect themselves from what they had been convinced was a threat to their livelihood. As well the division between workers and environmentalists played itself in other ways.

The disparities between Tofino, the home of "Friends of Clayoquot Sound" and the base for environmental protest, and the logging community of Ucluelet, are indicative of the split between the two groups. In 1999 the average home in Tofino cost $235,000 while the average in Ucluelet was $132,000. Tofino is a town of 1,283 people of whom over 200 earn more

---

[25] For an expose of the Forest Alliance hiring of Burson-Marstellar and Burson-Marstellar's less than illustrious clients, such as the Military Junta of Argentina, see Stephen Hume, "Forestry Flack's Record: Defending the Indefensible", *Vancouver Sun* Monday July 22 1991.and Stephen Hume, "Murder? Tortue? They Didn't See a Thing" *Vancouver Sun* Wednesday July 24 1991.

[26] For a short summary on the forest industry lobby and Share groups see *Talk and Log*, 31-42. For the story of how the *Vancouver Sun* shut down critical comments on Share see Kim Goldberg, "Axed: How the Vancouver Sun Became a Black Hole For Environmental Reporting" in *Witness to Wilderness: The Clayoquot Sound Anthology* Howard Breen-Needham et.al eds. (Vancouver: Arsenal Pulp Press,1994) 34-41. On the history of the Wise Use Movement in the United States see David Helvarg, The War Against the Greens: The Wise Use Movement, The New Right, and Anti-Environmental Violence (San Francisco: Sierra Club Books,1994).

[27] Canadian Library of Parliament, *Share Groups in British Columbia*, December 10 1991.

[28] Kim Goldberg, "More Wise Use Abuse MacMillan Bloedel Makes Use of Ron Arnold's Wise Use Movement" *Canadian Dimension* v.28(3) May/June, 1994 p.27.

than $50,000, while Ucluelet has 1,729 residents of whom 90 people make more than $50,000. Tofino currently has a 4.3 per cent unemployment rate compared to Ucluelet's 15.6 per cent.[29] Admittedly this illustrates different income but not necessarily class. When we look other indicators, however, they heighten the contrast of the towns. In Tofino 70 people work in primary industry; in Ucluelet, 155. Tofino has 30 people in manufacturing, Ucluelet 180. Tofino has 40 people in business services while Ucluelet has none. Tofino has 110 people in management occupations, Ucluelet 80. The levels of education differ substantially as well. In Tofino only 20 people have less than a grade nine educations, while the number in Ucluelet is 150. Tofino has 285 people who lack a high school diploma; Ucluelet, 345.[30] These statistics suggest the working-class nature of Ucluelet, and the more middle class, or professional managerial class, nature of Tofino, the base of the Friends of Clayoquot Sound and Greenpeace and the blockades of 1993. One caveat about the nature of class formation in the Clayoquot Sound area is that the Tofino area is not comprised simply of environmentalists and small to medium capitalist enterprises. The tourist firms do have employees who rely on the industry for their income. While these service sector workers immediate interests may not be the same as the forestry workers in Ucluelet, the climate of fear and uncertainty in resource towns would have been felt by these service sector workers as well. In the long run a sustainable forest economy that respected biological diversity would benefit both groups of workers. It could be around this issue that the individual interests could become collective interests and begin the formation of class solidarity.[31]

Workers who felt threatened by the scope of the anti-logging protests mobilized in a counter protest against the blockade. Over 5,000 people came from across BC to support the Clayoquot Sound strategy, and more specifically the logging community, in an event billed as "Ucluelet Rendezvous '93."[32] In counter-protest to the blockade, "200 litres of human excrement were dumped by the logging blockaders' information

[29] Stephen Hume, "Tofino and Ucluelet in a clash of cultures" *Vancouver Sun* (20 March, 1999). B1, B3.
[30] Statistics Canada, 1996 Census "Profile of Census and Subdivisions in British Columbia"
[31] Thanks to the anonymous reviewer who pointed out the complexities of class formation in Tofino that are not immediately apparent in the statistics.
[32] Stewart Bell, "Loggers, supporters confront protesters" *Vancouver Sun* (16 August 1993).

site."[33] Many environmental supporters would argue that this was merely industry-backed protest. While the working class groups that sprang up around this time were often industry supporters, they raised valid concerns that the workers felt environmentalists did not address. Failing to realize this was a great oversight on the environmentalists' part. By not engaging with workers concerns the situation was ripe for a backlash. One logger who had come from Williams Lake to support the Ucluelet workers put it this way. "People in forest dependent communities don't want to destroy the forests as environmentalists claim. But they also want their children to be able to work in the forest industry if they want to."[34] Unfortunately, industry supporters, such the BC Forestry Alliance, wanted to blame the environmentalists. The environmentalists were not the cause of the attrition of workers jobs over the past three decades. However, it was in the companies' interest to lay blame on the environmentalists.

Complicated issues were often simply reduced to sloganeering and generalizations. Des Kennedy, a Clayoquot defender, takes a position that at first seems sympathetic to working-class issues but quickly degenerates into anti-working-class rhetoric. Kennedy criticizes Share groups as "existing to protect capital, not workers."[35] While this would be true of the aims behind the corporate Share backers the workers in the groups were usually doing what they thought would best defend their jobs. Given the circumstances and the lack of dialogue between the workers and environmentalists this was not so unreasonable a tact to take. Lorelei Hanson points out that while there is "no doubt that corporate money helps fuel much of the activity of WUM [Wise Use Movement] the WUM should be recognized not just for the environmental setbacks they have caused, but also for the questions they raise concerning environmentally and economically sustainable livelihoods."[36] Unfortunately, Kennedy exacerbates the divide describing the average workers as dupes who are "caught in a vortex they do not understand" while "the more gullible

---

[33] William Boei, "200 litres of human excretement dumped at anti logging group's information tent." *Vancouver Sun* (4 August 1993) B2.

[34] Stewart Bell, "Loggers, supporters confront protesters" *Vancouver Sun* 16 August 1993.

[35] Des Kennedy, "Forest Industry Using Share to Dupe its Workers" *Witness to Wilderness: The Clayoquot Sound Anthology*. Howard Breen-Needham et.al eds. (Vancouver: Arsenal Pulp Press,1994), 156.

[36] Lorelei Hanson, "Turning Rivals into Allies :Understanding the Wise Use Movement", *Alternatives* v.21 (3) July/August, 1995

among them are easy prey for professional manipulators." [37] In contrast, he argues, "the campaign to save the Clayoquot rainforest is a classic example of non-violent civil disobedience. Participants maintain a friendly, open, and respectful attitude towards loggers, police, and company officials."[38] Kennedy insults the workers' intelligence, and then contrasts them with the benevolent 'classless' environmental group that harms no one. This simplistic argument ends up perpetuating the impasse between groups and does little to end the exploitation of workers or the environment

Race was another axis of oppression that tended to be ignored during the Clayoquot campaign. Repeating past mistakes with the Inuit during the sealing campaign Greenpeace entered into the forestry debate in the Sound without permission or consultation with the Nuu-Chah-Nulth peoples. Nelson Keitlah, co-chairman of the Nuu-Chah-Nulth central region Chiefs, stated, "We feel put off by people coming here who literally have nothing at stake. We are trying to create a better understanding and a new way of logging." For its part Greenpeace accused the forest companies of buying Nuu-Chah-Nulth support with promises of shared logging revenues.[39] This unfortunate lack of cultural sensitivity made any sort of 'peoples agenda' even more remote.[40]

As the protests eventually died down, Greenpeace spent the next year in a public relations war with the government and the BC Forest Alliance. Accusations were thrown back and forth all the way to Europe. The British Columbia government sent diplomatic groups over to show how the forest practices in BC were improving while Greenpeace and other environmental groups sent their members to counter the government's spin.[41] This was not new, as the government and protest groups had both traveled to Europe to present their cases before. It had, however, become the tactic of choice

---

[37] Kennedy, "Forest Industry," 156.

[38] Kennedy, "Forest Industry," 157.

[39] *Vancouver Sun* 22 June, 1996.

[40] In March 1994 the Clayoquot Sound Interim Measures Agreement was signed between the government and the Nuu-chah-nulth in Clayoquot Sound. This agreement allowed the cutting of 60,000 cubic meters of timber annually in an area comprising 1% of the Sound. A management board of five Nuu-Chah-Nulth and five government representatives was created. Any recommendations for logging or road building were to have the approval of a majority of its Nuu-Chah-Nulth members.

[41] *Globe and Mail*, "Harcourt Challenges Greenpeace" 2 February 1994; "BC ads Fight Greenpeace" *Globe and Mail* 11 February,1994. "BC Forest groups meets it match" *Globe and Mail* 30 March,1994.

for both groups after the confrontation in the summer of 1993.[42] This put the power over what would happen further away from the average worker or even the grassroots environmentalist. The debate was no longer even accessible to them.

The scientific panel continued to meet and issued its findings the same year. On Thursday 6 July 1995, the BC forests minister, Andrew Petter, and the environment minister, Elizabeth Cull, announced the New Democratic Party government had accepted all of the 127 recommendations by the scientific panel on Clayoquot Sound.[43] The principle recommendations included deferring logging until inventories of pristine areas had been done; reducing the annual allowable cut in the area, clearcuts reduced to four hectares; and conducting biological and cultural inventories to aid eco-based planning. Greenpeace was satisfied and agreed to call off its boycott of Macmillan Bloedel products. In June of 1999 Greenpeace announced that it would partner with Macmillan Bloedel to do the public relations work for its new logging methods in Clayoquot Sound. In exchange for MacMillan Bloedel respecting the Clayoquot Sound scientific panel's recommendations from 1995, Greenpeace would partner with Mac Blo to market its products. This was not a worker/green alliance. It was a meeting of two corporations: Greenpeace and MacMillan Bloedel.[44] The way in which Greenpeace sought to settle the dispute illustrates the Ehrenreichs' theory of Professional Managerial Class radicalism in action. The focus was on scientists and other experts providing a solution. Workers were not given expert status and were not

---

[42] "Forest minister 'greenwashing'; Replanting programs being trumpeted in Europe" *Times-Colonist* 6 October,1992.

[43] For the detailed findings see Scientific Panel for Sustainable Forest Practices in Clayoquot Sound, *Progress Report 2 : Review of Current Forest Practice Standards in Clayoquot Sound,* (Victoria, BC, 1994); Scientific Panel, *Report of the Scientific Panel for Sustainable Forest Practices in Clayoquot Sound,* (Victoria, BC, 1994); Scientific Panel, *A Vision and its Context: Global Context for Forest Practices in Clayoquot Sound,* (Victoria, BC, 1995); Scientific Panel, *First Nations' Perspectives Relating to Forest Practice Standards in Clayoquot Sound* (Victoria, BC, 1995); Scientific Panel, *Report 5: Sustainable Ecosystem Management in Clayoquot Sound: Planning and Practices.* (Victoria, BC, 1995) and for the government decision relating to the panel see Gordon Hamilton, "Clear-cut call on Clayoquot: Greenpeace puts MB boycott on hold" *Times-Colonist* 7 July 1995.

[44] *Vancouver Sun,* "MB, environmentalists agree to pact on Clayoquot logging" 16 June 1999 p.A3 "Green groups back logging" *The Province* 16 June 1999 p.A11 "Deal brings Clayoquot peace" *Times Colonist* 17 June 1999 p.A3.

involved in the solution at Clayoquot Sound. In the final analysis, despite its avowals of being beyond class interests, Greenpeace allied with the employers while an alliance with workers had not been fully explored and thus remained elusive. While this agreement could be seen as benefiting workers in that, at least potentially, it would increase sales and keep jobs stable, it has been shown that increased productivity is no guarantee of workers' job security. In fact, the company had a history of increasing production while conducting a reduction of the workforce. As well, the agreement was made above the heads of the workers and their union. Greenpeace's deal had nothing in it regarding the retaining of jobs and nothing in it for workers. It was purely a marketing agreement between companies.

CHAPTER FIVE

YES VIRGINIA, PROGRESSIVES BUST UNIONS TOO

Greenpeace has not had an easy relationship with unions in the woods or in their own backyard. At the same time that Greenpeace was failing to deal with workers in the forests or with their union, they were attempting to bust a homegrown union drive in their Toronto office. In June of 1993 headlines across Canada brought Greenpeace's internal conflict to public attention. The front page of the *Ottawa Citizen* read, "Greenpeace at War with Itself." The next day it was on the Canadian Press newswire and in newspapers across Canada. At issue was Greenpeace's attempt to break the union that had been formed by staff in the Toronto head office of Greenpeace Canada. The Greenpeace staff union filed a complaint with the Ontario labour relations board accusing Greenpeace of "bargaining in bad faith, using layoffs and other threats to intimidate union members, and of systemic discrimination against women and racial minorities."[1]

The newspaper reports focused on the allegations that Greenpeace was not using a large enough percentage of donations to go towards campaigns. This is not an insignificant issue. According to a leaked report Greenpeace was spending over ninety per cent of their money earned through donations on administration, not on campaigns. The spokesperson for Greenpeace admitted as much.[2] The fact that Greenpeace was not being honest about where its money was going reflects the unaccountable, undemocratic nature of the organization. However, it does not tell the whole story. What was underreported were the anti-union tactics Greenpeace was employing. This story came out in the alternative press when Bruce Livesey exposed the issue in the pages of *Canadian Dimension*. Greenpeace staffers formed a union, the Toronto Greenpeace

---

[1] "Greenpeace Canada at war with itself" *Ottawa Citizen* 9 June 1993, Canadian Press, "Greenpeace accused of betraying supporters: staff revolt rocks group" *Winnipeg Free Press* 10 June 1993 A3.
[2] "Greenpeace Canada at war with itself" *Ottawa Citizen* 9 June 1993

Staff Association, in December of 1992. Soon after, union organizers and union supporters began to be harassed and laid off. Two of the union organizers, Stan Gray and Gord Perks, were laid off. They claimed the layoffs were "a smokescreen for union busting."[3] Another staffer Andrea Ritchie stated that she "was laid off as part of the 'restructuring' that led to the lay-off of all campaign staff involved in organizing the union." In September of 1993, a Greenpeace worker who was a member of the union executive was fired without just cause. She was reinstated only after an appeal to the Ontario labour relations board ruled in the union's favour. It was after this incident that the union members went public. It also was revealed that Greenpeace had hired an anti-union law firm, Mathews, Dinsdale and Clark, best known as a defender of corporate polluters. They had, for example, defended Varnicolor Chemicals on a charge of illegally dumping toxic waste. Greenpeace hired Mathews, Dinsdale and Clark to bust the union and paid over $100,000 to the firm. It was the use of membership money to bust a union rather than support environmental campaigns that brought up the issue of budgeting priorities.[4] Brian Iler, a lawyer and member of Greenpeace, decided to cut his relationship with Greenpeace because of its union-busting campaign.

> As you are aware, I have been increasingly uncomfortable with Greenpeace management's approach to labour relations, and its apparent willingness to devote massive resources desperately needed by campaigns (and which were donated to Greenpeace in the expectation they would be used for campaigns) to oppose the legitimate and legal rights of your Toronto employees to form a union and to negotiate a collective agreement. I reject absolutely the defense that management had no alternative. Heavy-handed firings and refusal to accept seniority and other provisions absolutely standard in collective agreements indicate to me that management has indeed chosen the anti-union path.[5]

Ironically, the union-busting came at a time when it appeared Greenpeace was attempting to break with its past and move in a more pro-worker, pro-labour direction by hiring a liaison to work with labour.

---

[3] Bruce Livesey, "The Green Giant in Hot Water: The Politics of Greenpeace," *Canadian Dimension* (August/September 1994), 8.

[4] Livesey, "The Green Giant," 7-12.

[5] Letter from Brian Iler of Iler and Campbell to Joanne Dufay, Chair Greenpeace Canada, May 6 1994. Reprinted in *Canadian Dimension* (August/September 1994), 12.

Greenpeace had hired union activist Stan Gray in 1990 to work in a coalition with labour groups. Gray played a large role in creating the Green Work Alliance in 1991. Gray received a Ph.D. in politics at Oxford and held a teaching post at McGill from 1967-1970. He was a member of the socialist pro-independence group *Front de liberation populaire* and was fired from McGill and interned for three weeks during the FLQ crisis of 1970. He then suddenly left Montreal and ended up in Hamilton, Ontario, working at Westinghouse after being blacklisted from teaching. Gray worked there for ten years and was a workers' advocate on the health and safety committee.[6] At the time he was hired by Greenpeace, Stan Gray was running a union-funded health and safety centre called the Ontario Workers' Health Centre. His project at Greenpeace, The Green Work Alliance, was a coalition of environmental groups and union and labour activists whose slogan was, "Green Jobs Not Pink Slips."[7] Gray, a key organizer of the unionizing effort at Greenpeace, was fired allegedly due to restructuring. Greenpeace then pulled out of the Green Work Alliance.

The attitudes of Greenpeace towards labour would come to light in a very public fashion. At the Canadian Labour Congress convention in January 1994, executive director of Greenpeace Canada Jean Moffat stated, "Greenpeace has always worked with labour."[8] This enraged labour activist and former Greenpeace researcher Andrea Ritchie who

> leapt to her feet to chastise Moffat, telling the crowd about Greenpeace's attempts to bust the environmental organization's Toronto staff union, using an infamous management-side law firm to conduct first contract negotiations, and firing or laying off supporters.[9]

Ritchie made her comments "to point out the irony of Greenpeace speaking on building labour-environmental alliances given its political and internal track record."[10] Greenpeace's record is less surprising when one considers the class position of its founders and leadership and how their position is not meant to fundamentally challenge capital.

Greenpeace's trouble with unions continued into the 21st century. The anti-union activity of the 1990s was not entirely successful for Greenpeace management. Stan Gray who had been fired for attempting to unionize

---

[6] Bill Freeman, "Re-enter Stan Gray" *Our Generation* 16 (1983), 30-34.
[7] Stan Gray, "Democracy, Jobs & the Environment" *Canadian Dimension* (Nov-Dec 1992), 17-20.
[8] Livesey, "The Green Giant in Hot Water" 7.
[9] Livesey, "The Green Giant in Hot Water" 7.
[10] Andrea Ritchie, "Letter to the Editor", *Canadian Dimension* 28:6 (1994/1995).

successfully negotiated the first contract for his fellow workers in the
Greenpeace Toronto office. He filed an unfair dismissal suit at the Labour
Relations Board. Gray was rehired by Greenpeace on the condition he
resign and collect severance.[11] In addition the door to door canvassers and
telephone canvassers had successfully unionized with Office and Professional
Employees International Union (OPEIU) local 343. The first collective
agreement was signed in October 2001 and was set to expire in December
of 2003. Greenpeace's Toronto office shut down the door to door canvas
in the middle of the collective agreement. The employees claimed they had
been locked out by Greenpeace Management. Peter Tabuns who was the
executive director at the time stated, ""We extended an offer to everyone
in the door campaign,' he says, giving employees phone jobs with
"comparable salary and benefits."[12] Greenpeace insisted they were simply
exercising management rights to close a part of their operation. The
unionized canvassers saw it as management breaking a contract. They
stated that the phone campaign was completely different. "Contrary to
what management claims, Cooper says the phone positions offer fewer
hours than the door-to-door work and therefore don't have the same pay
rate or benefits. This loss of hours for full-time canvassers has become the
main issue. Only part-time positions will be available to phone canvassers.
Gary Connolly, the union steward, says this would represent a pay cut for
all of us."[13] The workers also claimed that Greenpeace was attempting to
renegotiate the collective agreement which was why they claimed they
were locked out, not laid off.

According to *Now Magazine*, "Patty Clancy from OPEIU says
Greenpeace met with the union in July to discuss the potential changes and
had agreed to further talks. But Greenpeace's next move was to serve
notice that the door-to-door campaign was shutting down."[14] The
contention of local 343 was that the decision to close the door canvas only
occurred after Greenpeace could not reopen the contract in the middle of
the life of the collective agreement. They cite that the non-union door
canvas in Montreal remained open and that Greenpeace Canada continued
to use non-union third party agencies to canvass in other cities. Non union

---

[11] Sharon Boase, "Gray's Labour of Love is Fighting for Workers: Won't Rest
Until Justice is Served" *The Spectator* (Hamilton Ontario, August 27 1997) A.1.
[12] Heather Campbell, "Pickets Pound Greenpeace" *NOW* Vol 22 No 10, November
7-14, 2002.
[13] Heather Campbell, "Pickets Pound Greenpeace" *NOW* Vol 22 No 10, November
7-14, 2002.
[14] Heather Campbell, "Pickets Pound Greenpeace" *NOW* Vol 22 No 10, November
7-14, 2002.

labour and contracting out is not limited to Greenpeace Canada. Greenpeace USA contracts out their door to door canvas to the Fund for Public Interest Research. In 2002 two workers for the Fund's LA Greenpeace Project filed complaints to the State's Labor Board and when they told their employer they were going to unionize the office was summarily closed within the week.[15] The title of the article that documented the union busting efforts sums up the problem; Union Busting: Progressives can do it too. The problem is that being progressive has become almost meaningless when dealing with workers issues. Almost any issue group can claim to be progressive but when it comes to working with unions or their own workers progressive does not seem to matter very much. In the Greenpeace Canada Toronto offices case, the issue did not go away. Peter Taubans, who was executive director of Greenpeace Canada at the time of the Greenpeace door to door canvassers' unionization, ran for the Ontario NDP leadership in 2009. COPE 343 (OPEIU Canada separated from the international to form the independent Canadian Office and Professional Employees Union, COPE) apparently supported one of Tabuns rivals Michael Prue. The issue of the Greenpeace canvas came up in the debate. COPE 343's only mention of the matter that is still available is thus;

> In our January 23, 2009 letter to the Michael Prue Leadership Campaign, a reference was made to the 'lockout' of Greenpeace Canada Door Canvass staff. This was not accurate. The circumstances surrounding the closure of the door canvass were amicably resolved as between Greenpeace and the Union, COPE Local 343, formerly OPE1U Local 343. COPE Local 343 regrets any inconvenience caused to Greenpeace by this error. COPE Local 343 and Greenpeace continue to have an amicable working relationship.[16]

It remains to be seen how well the relationship continues. Greenpeace Toronto remains unionized unlike most of Greenpeace Canada's operations however the door to door canvas was discontinued only to be started up under another name. In another seemingly positive development the forestry unions in Ontario have joined forces with Greenpeace.

Forestry unions in Ontario signed off on a report entitled "Building a Green Economy in the Boreal Forest." The core suggestions that found union support were a call for value-added forestry, community based forestry initiatives, and transition funding for a struggling industry.[17]

---

[15] Ben Ehrenreich, Busting Unions: Progressives Can Do It Too" *LA Weekly*, February 2002.

[16] COPE Local 343 - Press Release TORONTO, Feb. 24

[17] Sara Teitelbaum, *Building a Green Economy in the Boreal Forest* (Toronto:

Unlike what happened in B.C. it seems Greenpeace has managed to get
both workers and the employers on board. "I don't know if we've ever been
in a room with the unions and had industry support as well," said
Greenpeace's boreal campaigner, Catharine Grant. "We all realize
something has to give here and everyone recognizes we have to go greener
and protect jobs. I feel pretty hopeful from that perspective that we're
starting to get support from key stakeholders."[18] It is still early times in the
alliance and the Minister of Northern Development, Mines and Forestry
Michael Gravelle was using a familiar spin that makes one wonder how
long the agreement would last. He stated, "It is always great to get
feedback from all parties interested in our forests as we continue to move
forward together to work towards our similar goals. We will soon be
announcing our new model for forest tenure. In the meantime and in the
future, I look forward to further feedback and input from Greenpeace."[19] It
is noticable that he made no mention of workers or their union. Not to be
too cynical a positive development to add credence to the idea that this
alliance may work Greenpeace did unveil the report in the Communications,
Energy and Paperworkers Union hall in Thunder Bay, Ontario. The CEP
was being cautious, Kim Ginter, the CEP vice president noted, "What
we're supporting the report on is the green jobs part of it. I don't support
everything Greenpeace does, but I truly have to support the part of
creating jobs."[20] He added that "Provincial and federal governments need
to take immediate concrete steps to stimulate the forestry sector so
northwestern families can continue working in their communities.
Building a Green Economy shows both governments how to take these
steps."[21] While it is hard not to be skeptical of a possible alliance between
Greenpeace and forestry workers given the example of Clayoquot Sound if
cooperation is to happen then there has to be a first step and this requires
some amount of trust. Given my argument has been that Greenpeace and
other new social movement groups need to take more heed of class issues
and attempt to work in alliance with the working-class, rather than

Greenpeace Canada, November 2010).
[18] John Thompson, "Greenpeace's forestry strategy starting to gain support from
key stakeholders — both unions and industry" *Kenora Daily Miner and News*
[19] John Thompson, "Greenpeace's forestry strategy starting to gain support from
key stakeholders — both unions and industry" *Kenora Daily Miner and News*
[20] Kris Ketonen, "Greenpeace hits mark on forest: union" The Chronicle Journal
Saturday, November 20, 2010
[21] "Paperworkers' union supports Greenpeace's suggestions to stimulate northern
forestry" *Pulp and Paper Canada* Thunder Bay, Ont. Nov 30, 2010

negotiate with corporations while excluding working-class interests, it hardly seems fair to criticize their attempt in Ontario.

Greenpeace's history shows it is not a model for class conscious environmentalism. However, unions should also take some responsibility for this. Most unions in North America have clauses in their constitutions that ensure that goods and services needed while conducting union business are purchased from companies who employ union labour. For example, union conferences are held in union hotels and any printing is done in by unionized print shops. The promotion of buying union is integral to the sustainability of a vibrant union movement. Why then do union leaders not insist on working only with unionized groups amongst new social movements? The simple answer would be that they would not be able to work with many new social movements at all if they had this stipulation. I would suggest this is part of the problem. The onus is put on labour to be more progressive by new social movement theorists and activists yet very little pressure is put on new social movements themselves to improve their own labour record. The suggestion is that unions are the ones holding back new social movement progress: that somehow unions' ideas of defending working class interests are archaic. Perhaps it is time for the labour movement to challenge new social movements to meet the union movements' standards of solidarity and not let one issue social movements dictate what it means to be progressive. Writer Kim Goldberg recognizes the potential that alliances between environmentalists and unions represent. However, while Goldberg recognizes the merit of agreements like Tin Wis et al, "Occasionally the more politically enlightened elements within BC's labour and environmental movements manage to create small, demilitarized zones through grassroots alliances like the Tin-Wis Coalition, Save Georgia Strait Alliance, Peace in the Woods agreement, the South Island Forest Accord and the West Kootenay Forest Accord."[22] She also points out that, "while these undertakings are both significant and promising, they are nowhere near achieving critical mass, and their output has so far been limited to documents and good vibes rather than any measurable change to the present configuration of power and capital."[23] Goldberg rightly argues that the configuration of power and capital in society is not going to be

---

[22] Kim Goldberg, "Mac-Blo's tree." *Canadian Dimension* 26.n3 (April-May 1992): 28(1). CPI.Q (Canadian Periodicals). Gale. Simon Fraser University. 10 Dec. 2009

[23] Kim Goldberg, "Mac-Blo's tree." *Canadian Dimension* 26.n3 (April-May 1992): 28(1). CPI.Q (Canadian Periodicals). Gale. Simon Fraser University. 10 Dec. 2009

dislodged by a few agreements. However, capitalism is not monolithic and there are cracks and ruptures in the edifice of this economic system. What Tin Wis, the South Island Forest Accord, and the West Kootenay Forest Accord illustrate is that it is possible to link the struggle of loggers and environmentalists, and conflicts between the two are neither desirable nor inevitable. How many of these cracks in capitalism will be needed to either eliminate capitalism or transform it to a more equitable system is unknown. What is clear is that a counter hegemonic bloc can only be formed by knowingly and purposefully confronting the contradictions of capitalism. So far most new social movements have failed to do this. However, even though such alliances are difficult to form and maintain, we must continue to try.

Chapter Six

A Return to Class

This case study of specific Greenpeace campaigns illustrates that we cannot accept an interpretation of Greenpeace as a classless social movement capable of advancing an environmentalist agenda in everyone's interest. Greenpeace's undemocratic and unrepresentative nature also provokes questions about new social movements that have traditionally been leveled at labour. To continue to be critical of a labour movement without holding new social movements to similar standards can only entrench the mutual hostility that was so damaging to a successful alliance of workers and environmentalists in the case studies in this book.

This book also illustrates, using the case of the anti-sealing campaign, that Greenpeace pursued a course consistent with the idea of a PMC radicalism that rode roughshod over the interests of workers. Greenpeace attempted to impose its own solution on the sealing industry regardless of the effects on workers in the industry. This solution excluded the actual communities affected in favour of its own vision. It privileged the opinions of bureaucrats, planners, and experts of various sorts over the voices and opinions of the sealers. This anti-working class radicalism was not inevitable. However in order to forge a truly democratic counter-hegemonic bloc Greenpeace would need to address their PMC bias. They could then enter into dialogue with labour and working class groups on an equal footing and not act arbitrarily without consultation. Dismissing the transformative potential of the working class in theory can lead to an *a priori* justification for a practice that only entrenches mutual distrust on both sides. This allows companies and pro-business lobby groups to successfully use a bait and switch tactic that keeps workers and environmentalists hostile to one another rather than looking at each other as potential allies.

The professional managerial class bias of Greenpeace limits its ability to pursue a successful coalition with labour. While it would be reductionist to claim that ideology could simply be read off class positions, it would be naive to argue that class is not a factor. Ignoring the role of the working class in the environmental movement is to lose the opportunity for a meaningful attack on capitalism's exploitation of labour *and* the environment.

While new social movements and identity politics have seemingly abandoned class, often the working class has advanced the interests of all members within it, including women and ethnic minorities, as well as working on many issues that the new social movement theorists and activists believe only they are capable of solving. In the early part of the twentieth century the Industrial Workers of the World (IWW) was advancing an agenda that was in many ways far ahead of its time. Star Rosenthal notes that the IWW "advocated both the organization of Asiatics and the active participation of women as leaders and members."[1] One prominent female member of the IWW had a counter-argument formulated to single issue politics as early as 1915. In a newspaper article titled "The IWW Call to Women," Elizabeth Gurley Flynn wrote,

> To us society moves in grooves of class, not sex. Sex distinctions affect us insignificantly and would less, but for economic differences. It is to those women who are wage earners, or wives of workers, that the IWW appeals. We see no basis in fact for feminist mutual interest, no evidence of natural "sex conflict", nor any possibility – nor present desirability – of solidarity among women alone. The success of our program will benefit workers, regardless of sex, and injure all who, without effort, draw profits for a livelihood."[2]

Workers' advocacy for the rights of all workers regardless of particular "identities" of skill, ethnicity, race, or gender was not limited to a brief period in the 1900s. Social unionism and community unionism is a reoccurring theme throughout North American working class history. Steven Penfold points out the importance of community mobilization and participation in Cape Breton coal towns in the 1920s:

> Strike activity is viewed not as centred primarily in the workplace, but as a process of community mobilization. There is ample reason to adopt such a definition of strike activities in the case of the Cape Breton coalfields, since it was not just workplace but the entire community that was... "besieged" by wage cuts, the presence of troops, and company and

---

[1]   Star Rosenthal, "Union Maids: Organized Women Workers in Vancouver 1900-1915," in *BC Studies,* 41, (1979), 38.

[2]   Elizabeth Gurley Flynn, "The IWW Call to Women (1915)," in Rosalyn Fraad Baxandall, ed., *Words on Fire: The Live and writing of Elizabeth Gurley Flynn* (New Brunswick and London:Rutgers University Press, 1987), 104.

provincial police.[3]

This is an important consideration when discussing the working class. While there is much debate about the difference between public and private spheres and how gender roles proscribe who acts and how in these realms, debates focused on gender alone can sometimes lose sight of how the working class comes together in defence of their mutual class interests.

This is not a defence of gender norms in the 1920s it is meant to illustrate the power of community action. This is a power that new social movement groups neglect when entering communities with their own vision and not working with the working class who are affected by their actions. As Penfold continues, "The domestic labour of women constituted one of the foundations of class struggle in the coal communities, and working-class women raised both their voices and their fists in the name of their class community."[4] It is this defence of community and shared class interest that is lost in the rush to embrace new social movements over working class organization. Promoting new social movements as the answer to environmental problems also fails to recognize that the working-class was waging environmental struggles long before Greenpeace was founded. Class based groups have been struggling for healthy, clean working environments at the site of production for more than a century. The struggle over parkland on Deadman's Island in Vancouver is an example of early environmental advocacy by Canadian workers.[5] In the United States of America, labour activists formed the Workers Health Bureau in 1921 to "research in adjunct to the union movement for health and safety."[6] The Bureau put forward a program that integrated labour and the environment with the understanding that, "Health is an industrial and class problem."[7] The United Steel Workers of America supported

---

[3] Steven Penfold, "Have You No Manhood in You? Gender and Class in the Cape Breton Coal Towns, 1920-1926," *Gender and History in Canada*, Joy Parr and Mark Rosenfeld eds. (Toronto:Copp Clark Ltd., 1996), 271.

[4] Penfold, Manhood, 288.

[5] The Deadman's Island struggle took place for a number of years, 1887-1889 and the Vancouver Trades and Labour Council originally supported it being held as parkland. For details of this see Mark Leier, *Red Flags and Red Tape,* 58-61. For more on the labour movement and environment at the turn of the century in Vancouver see Robert A.J. McDonald, "Holy Retreat or Practical Breathing Spot? Class Perceptions of Vancouver's Stanley Park, 1910-1913," *Canadian Historical Review* 64 (1984), 127-53.

[6] Robert Gottlieb, *Forcing the Spring: The Transformation of the American Environmental Movement* (Washington DC:Island Press, 1993), 69.

[7] Gottlieb, *Forcing the Spring,* 69.

environmental initiatives in the 1960s and 1970s and even negotiated health and safety language into their contracts. In one agreement with the U.S. Steel company plant in Clariton, Pennsylvania the steelworkers negotiated engineering controls that limited carcinogenic emissions from the coke ovens.[8] These examples illustrate how workers exercising power at the point of production transcends what Greenpeace might see as narrow class interests.

There are similar examples throughout Canadian labour history. Jerry Lembcke and William M. Tattam point out in their book, *One Union in Wood*, that, "under Communist editorship the IWA's paper, the *Timberworker,* opposed clearcutting of forests and log exports and promoted reforestation and conservation in the 1940s.[9] This was three decades before Greenpeace's opposition to clear cutting. The *Timberworker's* position makes sense, for workers stand to lose when technologies for faster, more profitable, and less environmentally sound logging are implemented. Of course they also lose when the environment collapses.[10]

During the time of ascendancy for new social movements, unions were actively fighting for environmental issues. In her article "Greening the Canadian Workplace: Unions and the Environment," Laurel Sefton MacDowell notes that

> throughout the 1970s and 1980s, as unions increasingly brought occupational health and safety matters to the bargaining table, the number of strikes over such issues increased, and unions allocated more staff, time, and money to reducing workplace hazards and disease.[11]

A good example of this occurred in 1970, when construction workers, hired to build a new mine for the company Utah of the Americas on northern Vancouver Island, called for a hearing into the ecological effects of their construction project even if it meant losing their jobs.[12] Attempts

---

[8] Gottlieb, *Forcing the Spring,* 272.

[9] Jerry Lembcke and William M. Tattam, *One Union in Wood: A Political History of the International Woodworkers of America* (BC:Harbour Publishing, 1984), 177.

[10] For a brief history on the IWA and environmental activism of its members see Chapter 6 of Andrew Neufeld and Andrew Parnaby, *The IWA in Canada: The Life and Times of an Industrial Union* (Vancouver:IWA Canada/New Star Books, 2000).

[11] Laurel Sefton MacDowell, "Greening the Canadian Workplace: Unions and the Environment," *Sustainability the Challenge: People, Power and the Environment* L. Anders Sandberg and Sverker Sorlin eds.. (Montreal:Black Rose Books, 1998), 168.

[12] Barry Culhane and Robin Harger, "Environment Vs. Jobs," *Canadian Dimension*

to have working relations would be desirable for both labour and environmental groups. Taking into account the positive contribution of workers to the environment would benefit any potential alliance.

Simply reasserting the primacy of class to counter the claims of new social movements that labour cannot act as an agent of progressive transformation would only exacerbate the mutual distrust between the different camps. However, recognition by both labour and environmentalists that they have shared concerns and a common enemy could lead to working relationships on many campaigns. Capitalism is not based on meeting the needs of the world's population but on profiting from exploiting labour *and* natural resources. Marx understood this over 150 years ago when he wrote that the bourgeoisie chased over the globe to constantly expand their markets and search for raw materials.[13] The results of this search for constant expansion are industries that, "no longer work up indigenous raw material, but raw material drawn from the remotest zones."[14] This is essentially a description of globalization and neither workers nor the environment benefit from this process. Richard Douthwaite challenges the idea that growth benefits workers in his book *The Growth Illusion*. Douthwaite succinctly tackles myths about the benefits of growth, arguing that as profits have gone up for industrialists, wages have gone down for workers and this has been accompanied by an inevitable destruction of the environment that results from rampant industrialism.[15] While Marx did not live to see the full global expansion of capital he did offer remedies. Jonathan Hughes suggests that some of the solutions to the current situation lie with Marx's communist slogan, "From each according to his ability, to each according to his needs."[16] This simple idea challenges overproduction, commodity fetishism, and the

---

9:5 (1973), 49.

[13] Karl Marx and Friedrich Engels, *The Communist Manifesto*, (New York:Penguin Books, 1985), 83.

[14] Marx and Engels, *The Communist Manifesto*, 83-84.

[15] Richard Douthwaite, *The Growth Illusion: How Economic Growth has Enriched the Few, Impoverished the Many and Endangered the Planet* (Gabriola Island, B.C.:New Society Publishers, 1999)

[16] Hughes discusses at length what Marx meant by this statement in his Critique of the Gotha Programme and argues against environmentalists' interpretation that this was a statement supporting abundant growth by Economic and Philosophical manuscripts and other works. For a full explanation of this see Jonathan Hughes, Ecology and Historical Materialism (Cambridge: Cambridge University Press, 2000) particularly Chapter 6 "Capitalism, Socialism and the Satisfaction of Needs," 161-200.

exploitation of surplus value of labour and environment for personal profit. This puts the interests of the capitalists in direct opposition to the interests of the working-class and the environmental movement.

An excellent contemporary example of how workers and environmentalists can mobilize together was the activism of IWW member and Earth First! organizer Judi Bari. In the late 1980s and early 1990s Judi Bari challenged the radical environmental movement to address class issues by forging an alliance with the revolutionary syndicalism of the IWW to oppose logging in the California redwood forests. Bari was so successful that she convinced a whole faction of Earth First!, called Ecotopia EarthFirst!, to renounce tree spiking which increased her credibility with mill workers in the Pacific Northwest.[17] More recently, in the spirit of the Battle of Seattle, members of the IWW and Earth First! joined forces to support striking sheet metal workers at Kaiser Aluminum in Washington State. Workers at Kaiser had been on strike against the company owned by Charlie Hurwitz's Maxxam Corporation, which also owns Pacific Lumber the logging operation cutting the redwoods forests of California. The worker environmentalists organized a picket line, a flotilla picket and a banner hanging at the Port of Tacoma where scab labour was to unload a shipment of ore. The ship was stopped from unloading and had to remain in port for twenty-four days rather than the typical seven.[18] This kind of action and the efforts of some Earth Firsters! and the IWW shows the potential for a truly united struggle that addresses the interconnectedness of labour and the environment. The EF! Report on the IWW/EF!/Steelworker alliance sums up some of the ideas in this article and the reasons why an enviro-worker alliance is logical. "When you have Charles Hurwitz exploiting both his workers and the land, it's a natural coalition."[19] A coalition between workers and environmentalists is a necessary coalition if one wants to stop the exploitation of workers and the land, but it is not as

---

[17] For more on Judi Bari's ideas see Judi Bari *Timber Wars* (Maine: Common Courage Press, 1994). On the FBI's COINTELPRO operations against Judi Bari see, Ward Churchill and Jim Vander Wall, *Agents of Repression: FBI Attacks on the Black Panthers and the American Indian Movement* (Boston: South End Press, 1988). On the case against the FBI brought by Judi Bari see "Judi Bari Court Victory", *Earth First! Journal* Yule 1997 and IWW Local No.1/Earth First! "Who Bombed Judi Bari" (Fort Bragg: Wobbly Bureau of Investigation, no date). Also see http://www.monitor.net/~bari.
[18] "Union/EF! Alliance Costs Hurwitz Half a Million," *Earth First! Journal* Vol.XXIV, No.III Feb-Mar (Brigid), 1999.
[19] "Union/EF! Alliance."

natural as it may seem. The mutually reinforced antagonism between workers and environmentalists needs to be addressed before a true coming together of Teamsters and Turtles can be achieved. This book is only the beginning of addressing such issues. Understanding the history of conflicts between workers and Greenpeace can be seen as a partial deterrent against further conflicts between class and environmental concerns. By examining Greenpeace's mistakes and missteps in their anti-sealing campaign, their forestry campaign in BC, and in its anti-union stance in Toronto, environmentalist and labour groups can attempt to learn from the past and forge new approaches to working together.

BIBLIOGRAPHY

Primary Sources

Annual Reports

Greenpeace Annual Review. Toronto: Greenpeace Foundation.
Greenpeace Canada. *Financial Statments*. Toronto: Greepeace Canada.

Government Publications

"An introduction to poverty in Canada," *The Canadian Fact book on Poverty*, Canadian Council on Social Development, 1996, http://www.cfc-efc.ca/docs
"Child and Family Canada: An Introduction to Poverty in Canada," *The Canadian Fact Book on Poverty*, Canadian Council on Social Development, 1996, http://www.ccsd.ca/pcc97hl.htm
"Highlights," *The Progress of Canada's Children*, 1997, http://www.ccsd.ca/pcc97hl.htm
Clayoquot Land Use Decision: Background Report (Victoria: Queen's Printer for British Columbia, 1993).
National Anti-Poverty Organization, *Poverty Statistics at a Glance*, http://www.napo-onap.ca/nf-glanc.htm
Office of the Premier, "Clayoquot Decision Balances Environmental, Economic and Social Values." News Release. Victoria, Province of BC, 13 April,1993.
Province of British Columbia, *Clayoquot Sound Land Use Decision: Key Elements* (Victoria: Province of British Columbia, April 1993).
Province of British Columbia, *The Government of British Columbia Response to the Commission on Resources and Environment's Public Report and Recommendations Regarding Issues Arising From the Clayoquot Land Use Decision.* (Victoria, BC: Province of British Columbia, 1993)
Scientific Panel for Sustainable Forest Practices in Clayoquot Sound, *Report 5 – Sustainable Ecosystem Management in Clayoquot Sound: Planning and Practices.* Victoria: Clayoquot Scientific Panel, 1995.
Scientific Panel for Sustainable Forest Practices in Clayoquot Sound,

Progress Report 2 : Review of Current Forest Practice Standards in Clayoquot Sound. (Victoria, BC: Clayoquot Scientific Panel, 1994.)

Scientific Panel for Sustainable Forest Practices in Clayoquot Sound, *Report of the Scientific Panel for Sustainable Forest Practices in Clayoquot Sound.* (Victoria, BC: Clayoquot Scientific Panel, 1994.)

Scientific Panel for Sustainable Forest Practices in Clayoquot Sound *A Vision and its Context : Global Context for Forest Practices in Clayoquot Sound* (Victoria, B.C: Cortex Consultants, 1995)

Scientific Panel for Sustainable Forest Practices in Clayoquot Sound, *First Nations' Perspectives Relating to Forest Practice Standards in Clayoquot Sound* (Victoria, BC: Cortex Consultants, 1995)

Scientific Panel for Sustainable Forest Practices in Clayoquot Sound (BC) *Report 5: Sustainable Ecosystem Management in Clayoquot Sound: Planning and Practices.* (Victoria, B.C : Clayoquot Scientific Panel, 1995.)

The Clayoquot Sound Sustainable Development Task Force, *Report to the Minister of Environment and the Minister of Regional and Economic Development.* (Victoria: The Task Force,1991).

Newspapers and Periodicals

Georgia Straight (Vancouver, BC)
Greenlink: Canadian Environmental Magazine (Vancouver, BC)
Greenpeace Canada Action
Greenpeace Chronicles (Vancouver, BC)
Greenpeace Examiner (Vancouver, BC)
Monday Magazine (Victoria, BC)
Ottawa Citizen
The Province (Vancouver, BC)
Times-Colonist (Victoria, BC).
Vancouver Sun

Secondary Sources

Articles

Adam, Barry D. "Post-Marxism and the New Social Movements." *The Canadian Review of Sociology and Anthropology* 30, (1993), 316-36.

Bagguley, Paul. "Social Change, the Middle Class and the Emergence of 'New Social Movements': a Critical Analysis." *The Sociological Review* 40, (1992), 26-48.

Bakunin, Michael. "Preamble and Program of the International Alliance of the Socialist Democracy." In *Bakunin: on Anarchism*, ed. Sam Dolgoff, 426-428. Montreal: Black Rose Books, 1980.

Bryden, Ronald. "They Impale Bleeding Hearts Don't They?" *Macleans* (20-27 March 1978), 91.

Burda, Cheri, Fred Gale, and Michael M'Gonigle. "Eco-Forestry Versus the State(us) Quo: Or Why Innovative Forestry is Neither Contemplated Nor Permitted Within the State Structure of British Columbia." *BC Studies* 119 (1998), 45-72.

Burda, Cheri, Fred Gale, and Michael M'Gonigle. "Reply." *BC Studies* 119 (1998), 82-86.

Callinicos, Alex. "The 'New Middle Class' and Socialist Politics." *International Socialism* 2:20 (1985), 104.

Carroll, William K. and R. S. Ratner. "Master Framing and Cross-movement Networking in Contemporary Social Movements." *The Sociological Quarterly* 37, (1996), 601-625.

Carroll, William K. and R. S. Ratner. "Media Strategies and Political Projects: A Comparative Study of Social Movements." *Canadian Journal of Sociology* 24:1 (1999). 1-34.

Carroll, William K. and R. S. Ratner. "Old Unions and New Social Movements." *Labour /Le Travail* 35 (1995), 195-221.

Charlton, John. "Talking Seattle." *International Socialism* 86, (2000).

Church, Michael. "Commentary." *BC Studies* 119 (1998), 78-82.

Cockburn, Alexander. "Trade Wars, Trade Truths." *The Nation* 20, (1999).

Culhane, Barry and Robin Harger. "Environment Vs. Jobs." *Canadian Dimension* 9:5 (1973), 49.

D'Anieri, Paul, Claire Ernest, and Elizabeth Kier. "New Social Movements in Historical Perspective." *Comparative Politics* 22:4 (1990), 445-458.

Duncan, Sandy Frances. "Solidarity." In *Witness to Wilderness: The Clayoquot Sound Anthology*. eds. Howard Breen-Needham et al. Vancouver: Arsenal Pulp Press, 1994.

Eder, Klaus. "The New Social Movements: Moral Crusades, Political Pressure Groups, of Social Movements?" *Social Research* 53:4 (1985), 869-890.

—. "Green Politics and the New Class." *Political Studies* 37:2, (1989), 205-223.

Ehrenreich, Barbara and John Ehrenreich. "The Professional-Managerial Class." *Radical America* 11:2, (1977), 7-32.

Ellis, Richard J. "Romancing the Oppressed: The New Left and the Left Out." *Review of Politics* 58, (1996), 109-154.

Flynn, Elizabeth Gurley. "The IWW Call to Women (1915)." *Words on Fire: The Live and Writing of Elizabeth Gurley Flynn.* ed. Rosalyn Fraad Baxandall. New Brunswick and London: Rutgers University Press, 1987.

Freeman, Bill. "Re-enter Stan Gray." *Our Generation* 16 (1983), 30-34.

Goldberg, Kim. "Axed: How the Vancouver Sun Became a Black Hole for Environmental Reporting." In *Witness to Wilderness: The Clayoquot Sound Anthology.* eds. Howard Breen-Needham et al. 34-41. Vancouver: Arsenal Pulp Press, 1994.

—. Letters to the Editor. *Canadian Dimension* 28:6 (1994/1995).

Gray, Stan. "Democracy, Jobs & the Environment." *Canadian Dimension. 26:8* (1992), 17-20.

—. "Labour's Environmental Challenge." *Canadian Dimension.* (August - September 1994), 13-16.

Gwyn, Sandra. "The Media go to the Seal Hunt: Radical Chic versus the Newfie Swilers." *Saturday Night,* 92:4 *(*1977), 26-29.

Hannigan, John A. "Alaine Touraine, Manuel Castells and Social Movement Theory: A Critical Appraisal." *The Sociological Quarterly* 26:4, (1985), 435-454.

Hirsch, Joachim. "The Crisis of Fordism, Transformations of 'Keynesian' Security State and the New Social Movements." *Research in Social Movements, Conflicts and Change* 10, 43-55.

Iler, Brian. Letter from Brian Iler of Iler and Campbell to Joanne Dufay, Chair Greenpeace Canada, May 6 1994. Reprinted in *Canadian Dimension* (August/September 1994), 12.

Inglis, Sarah. "McDonald's Union Drive-thru." *Our Times* (June/July 1994), 19-28.

Kennedy, Des. "Forest Industry Using Share to Dupe its Workers." In *Witness to Wilderness: The Clayoquot Sound Anthology.* eds. Howard Breen-Needham et al. Vancouver: Arsenal Pulp Press, 1994.

Kitschelt, Herbert. "'New Social Movements in West Germany and the United States." *Political Power and Social Theory* 5:310, (1985).

Klein, Naomi. "Salesgirl Solidarity." *This Magazine* 28:6, (1995), 12-19.

Livesey, Bruce. "The Green Giant in Hot Water: The Politics of Greenpeace." *Canadian Dimension.* 28:4, (1994), 7-12.

Loewen, Gary. "The Changing Face of Poverty." *Canadian Mennonite* 2:10 (1998), 12-13.

Lowe, Graham. S. "Mechanization, Feminization, and Managerial Control in the Early Twentieth-Century Canadian Office." In *On The Job: Confronting the Labour Process in Canada.* eds Craig Heron and Robert Storey, 177-209. Kingston; Montreal: McGill-Queen's

University Press, 1986.

MacDowell, Laurel Sefton. "Greening the Canadian Workplace: Unions and the Environment." *Sustainability the Challenge: People, Power and the Environment,* eds. L. Anders Sandberg and Sverker Sorlin, 167-176. Montreal: Black Rose Books, 1998.

Magnusson, Warren and Rob Walker. "De-Centring the State: Political Theory and Canadian Political Economy." *Studies in Political Economy.* 26, (1988), 37-71.

Marchak, Patricia. "Commentary." *BC Studies* 119 (1998), 73-78.

Marx, Karl. "Value, Price and Profit." In *Wage-Labour and Capital: Value, Price and Profit.* 1-62. New York: International Publishers, 1988.

McDonald, Robert A.J. "Holy Retreat or Practical breathing Spot ? Class Perceptions of Vancouver's Stanley Park, 1910-1913." *Canadian Historical Review* 64 (1984), 127-53.

Melucci, Alberto. "A Strange Kind of Newness: What's 'New' in New Social Movements?" In *New Social Movements: From Ideology to Identity*, eds. Enrique Larana, Hank Johnston, and Joseph R. Gusfield, 101-130. Philadelphia: Temple University Press, 1994.

Mooers, Colin and Alan Sears. "The 'New Social Movements' and the Withering Away of State Theory." In *Organizing Dissent: Contemporary Social Movements in Theory and Practice.* ed. William K. Carroll. Victoria: Garamond Press, 1992.

Nelson, Joyce. "Technology, Not Environmentalism Cuts Forest Jobs." *Witness to Wilderness: The Clayoquot Sound Anthology.* eds. Howard Breen-Needhame et al. Vancouver: Arsenal Pulp Press, 1994.

Offe, Claus. "New Social Movements: Challenging the Boundaries of Institutional Politics." *Social Research* 52:4, (1985), 817-868.

Penfold, Steven. "Have You No Manhood in You? Gender and Class in Cape Breton Coal Towns, 1920-1926." In *Gender and History in Canada*, eds. Joy Parr and Mark Rosenfeld, 270-293. Toronto: Copp Clark, 1996.

Pinkerton, Evelyn W. "Co-Management Efforts as Social Movements: The Tin Wis Coalition and the Drive for Forest Practices Legislation in British Columbia." *Alternatives* 19:3, (1993), 33-35.

Resnick, Philip. "Social Democracy in Power: The Case of British Columbia." *BC Studies* 34, (1977), 3-20.

Ritchie, Andrea. "Letter to the Editor", *Canadian Dimension* 28:6 (1994/1995).

Robinson, Randy. "Big Mac's Counter Attack." *Our Times* (June/July 1994), 29-30.

Rogers, Nicholas, Bryan Palmer, and Ellen Meiksins Wood. "Edward Palmer Thompson: In Memoriam." *Studies in Political Economy* 43, (1994), 7-32.

Rosenthal, Star. "Union Maids: Organized Women Workers in Vancouver 1900-1915." *B C Studies* 41, (1979), 36-55.

Scott, Joan. "The Evidence of Experience." *Critical Inquiry* 17 (1991), 773-797.

Steinmetz, George. "Regulation Theory, Post-Marxism, and the New Social Movements." *Comparative Studies in Society and History* 36:1, (1994), 176-212.

Sweeny, Robert C. H. "The Staples as the Significant Past: A Case Study in Historical Theory and Method." In *Canada: Theoretical Discourse/ Discourse Theoriques,* eds. Terry Goldie, Carmen Lambert and Roland Lorimer, 327-349. Montreal: 1994.

Travers, Ray. "History of Logging and Sustained Yield in BC, 1911-90." *Forests Planning Canada* 8:1 (1992).

Travers, Ray. "History of Logging and Sustained Yield in BC, 1911-90." *Forests Planning Canada* 8:1 (1992).

Wakeman, Bob. "Those Damned Seal Again." *Macleans* (January 1978), 21.

Wenzel, George. "The Harp-seal Controversy and the Inuit Economy," *Arctic* 31:1, (1978), 3-6.

Wilde, Lawrence. "Class Analysis and the Politics of New Social Movements." *Capital & Class* 42, (1990), 55-78.

Williams, Karen. "Chain Reactions." *Our Times* (June/July 1994), 31-33.

Wood, Ellen Meiksins. "A Tale of Two Democracies." *History Today* 44:5 (1994), 50-55.

—. "Back to Marx," *Monthly Review* 49:2 (1997), 1-9.

—. "Labor, the State, and Class Struggle," *Monthly Review* 49:3, (1997), 1-17.

—. "Modernity, Postmodernity, or Capitalism?" *Monthly Review* 48:3 (1996), 21-39.

—. "Rational Choice Marxism: Is the Game Worth the Candle?" *New Left Review* 177, (1989), 41-88.

—. "Viewpoint: The Left's Identity Crisis." *In These Times*, 18:15 (1994), 28-29.

—. "What is the 'Postmodern' Agenda? An Introduction," *Monthly Review,* 47:3 (1995), 1-12.

Wood, Ellen Meiksins and John Bellamy Foster. "Marxism and Postmodernism: A Reply to Roger Burbach." *Monthly Review* 47, (1996), 41-46.

Books

Adams, Howard. *A Tortured People: The Politics of Colonization.* Penticton: Theytus Books, 1995.

Adkin, Laurie E. *The Politics of Sustainable Development: Citizens, Unions and the Corporations.* Montreal; New York: Black Rose Books, 1998.

Althusser, Louis. *Lenin and Philosophy and Other Essays.* Ben Brewster, trans. London: New Left Books, 1971.

Armstrong, Pat and Hugh Armstrong. *The Double Ghetto: Canadian Women and their Segregated Work.* Toronto: McClelland & Stewart, 1994.

Aron, Raymond. *The Elusive Revolution: Anatomy of a Student Revolt.* Trans. Gordon Clough, New York: Praeger Publishers, 1969.

Bakunin, Micheal. *Bakunin: on Anarchism.* Ed. and trans, Sam Dolgoff, Montreal: Black Rose Books, 1980.

Boggs, Carl. *Social Movements and Political Power: Emerging Forms of Radicalism in the West..* Philadelphia: Temple University Press, 1986.

Bohlen, Jim. *Making Waves: The Origins and Future of Greenpeace.* Montreal: Black Rose Books, 2001.

Bookchin, Murray. *Remaking Society.* Montreal: Black Rose Books, 1989.

Bowles Samuel and Herbert Gintis. *Democracy and Capitalism: Property, Community, and the Contradictions of Modern Social Thought.* New York: Basic Books, 1986.

Briskin, Linda, and Patricia McDermott. *Women Challenging Unions: Feminism, Democracy, and Militancy.* Toronto: University of Toronto Press, 1993.

Brown, Michael and John May. *The Greenpeace Story.* Scarborough Ont.: Prentice-Hall Canada, 1989.

Cadigan,Sean T. *Hope and Deception in Conception Bay: Merchant-Settler Relations in Newfoundland, 1785-1855.* Toronto: University of Toronto Press, 1995.

Candow, James E. *Of Men and Seals: A History of the Newfoundland Seal Hunt.* Ottawa: Ministry of the Environment, 1989.

Cantor, Milton. *The Divided Left: American Radicalism 1900-1975.* New York: Hill and Wang, 1978.

Carroll, William K, ed. *Organizing Dissent: Contemporary Social Movements in Theory and Practice.* Rev. ed. Toronto: Garamond Press, 1997.

—. *Corporate Power and Canadian Capitalism.* Vancouver: University of British Columbia Press, 1986.

Carter, Bob. *Capitalism, Class Conflict, and the New Middle Class.* London: Routledge & Kegan Paul, 1985.

Cohn-Bendit, Daniel and Gabriel Cohn-Bendit. *Obsolete Communism The Left-Wing Alternative.* Arnold Pomerans, trans.. New York: McGraw-Hill Book Company, 1968.

Dale, Stephen. *McLuhan's Children: The Greenpeace Message and the Media.* Toronto: Between the Lines, 1990.

Dalton, Russell and Manfred Kuechler, eds. *Challenging the Political Order.* New York: Oxford University Press, 1990.

Darling, Craig. *In Search of Consensus: An Evaluation of the Clayoquot Sound Sustainable Development Task Force Process.* Victoria: University of Victoria Institute for Dispute Resolution, 1991.

Douthwaite, Richard. *The Growth Illusion: How Economic Growth has Enriched the Few, Impoverished the Many and Endangered the Planet.* Rev. ed. Gabriola Island, BC: New Society Publishers, 1999.

Drushka, Ken. *HR: A Biography of H.R. MacMillan.* Madeira Park BC: Harbour Publishing, 1995, 184.

—. *Working in the Woods: A History of Logging on the West Coast.* (Madeira Park, BC: Harbour Publishing, 1992).

Drushka, Ken and Hannu Konttinen. *Tracks in the Forest: The Evolution of Logging Machinery.* Helsinki, Finland: Timberjack Group Oy, 1997.

Eagleton, Terry. *Ideology: An Introduction.* London; New York: Verso, 1991.

Eder, Klaus. *The New Politics of Class: Social Movements and Cultural Dynamics in Advanced Societies.* London; Newbury Park, CA: Sage Publications, 1993.

Forgacs, David, ed. *An Antonio Gramsci Reader.* New York: Schocken Books, 1988.

Freeman, Jo. "The Tyranny of Structurelessness." *Untying the Knot: Feminism, Anarchism & Organization.* London: Dark Star Press and Rebel Press, 1984.

Georgakas, Dan and Marvin Surkin. *Detroit: I Do Mind Dying, a Study in Urban Revolution.* Cambridge, Massachusts: South End Press, 1998.

German, Lindsey. *A Question of Class.* London: Bookmarks, 1996.

Gottlieb, Robert. *Forcing the Spring: The Transformation of the American Environmental Movement.* Washington, DC: Island Press, 1993.

Gouldner, Alvin. *Against Fragmentation: The Origins of Marxism and the Sociology of Intellectuals.* Oxford: Oxford University Press, 1985.

Griffin, Sean, ed. *Fighting Heritiage: Highlights of the 1930s Struggle for Jobs and Militant Unionism in British Columbia.* Vancouver: Tribune Publishing,

Gurr, Ted. *Why Men Rebel.* Princeton, NJ: Princeton University Press, 1970.

Habermas, Jurgen. *The Theory of Communicative Action.* Vol. 2. Boston: Beacon Halfmann, Jost, 1987.

Hak, Gordon. *Turning Trees into Dollars: The British Columbia Coastal Lumber Industry 1858-1913.* Toronto: University of Toronto Press, 2000.

Henke, Janice Scott. *Seal Wars: An American Viewpoint.* St. John's, Nfld: Breakwater, 1985.

Heron, Craig. *The Canadian Labour Movement: A Short History.* 2nd Edition. Toronto: Lorimer, 1996.

Hobsbawm, E.J. *Primitive Rebels: Studies in Archaic Forms of Social Movement in the Nineteenth and Twentieth Centuries.* New York: W.W.Norton and Company, 1959.

Hunter, Robert. *Warriors of the Rainbow: A Chronicle of the Greenpeace Movement.* New York: Holt, Rinehart and Winston, 1979.

Johnson, Chalmers. *Revolutionary Change.* Boston: Little Brown, 1966.

Katsisficas, George. *The Subversion of Politics: European Autonomous Social Movements and the Decolonization of Everyday Live.* New Jersey: Humanities Press, 1997.

Krantz, Frederick. ed. *History From Below: Studies in Popular Protests and Popular Ideology in Honour of George Rudé.* Montreal: Concordia University, 1985.

Laclau, Ernesto. *New Reflections on the Revolution of Our Time.* Jon Barnes, trans. London; New York: Verso, 1990.

Laclau, Ernesto and Chantal Mouffe. *Hegemony and Socialist Strategy: Towards a Radical Democratic Politics.* Winston Moore and Paul Cammack, trans.. London: Verso, 1985.

Lamson, Cynthia. *Bloody Decks and a Bumper Crop: The Rhetoric of Sealing Counter-Protest.* St. John's, Nfld: Institute of Social and Economic Research, Memorial University of Newfoundland, 1979.

Laxer, James. *In Search of a New Left: Canadian Politics After the NeoConservative Assault.* Toronto: Viking, 1996.

Laxer, James. *The [Undeclared] War: Class Conflict in the Age of Cyber Capitalism.* Toronto: Viking, 1998.

Leier, Mark. *Red Flags and Red Tape: The Making of a Labour Bureaucracy.* Toronto: University of Toronto Press, 1995.

Lembcke, Jerry and William M. Tattam, *One Union in Wood: A Political History of the International Woodworkers of America.* BC: Harbour Publishing, 1984.

M'Gonigle, Michael, and Ben Parfitt. *Forestopia: A Practical Guide to the*

New Forest Economy. Madeira Park, BC: Harbour Publishing, 1994.

MacIssac, Ron and Anne Champagne, eds. *Clayoquot Mass Trials: Defending the Rainforest.* Gabriola Island, BC: New Society Publishers, 1994.

Macqueen, Diane Leigh Marie. "Consensus Based Decision-making: The Clayoquot Sound Steering Committee Process." MA Thesis, Simon Fraser University, Burnaby, BC, 1996.

Magnusson, Warren, et al., eds.. *After Bennett: A New Politics for British Columbia.* Vancouver: New Star Books, 1986.

Marchak, Patricia M., Scott L. Aycock and Deborah M. Herbert. *Falldown: Forest Policy in British Columbia.* Vancouver: David Suzuki Foundation and Ecotrust Canada,1999.

Marx, Karl and Friedrich Engels. *The Communist Manifesto.* New York : Penguin Books, 1985.

McGuigan, Gerald F. ed. *Student Protest.* Toronto: Methuen Publications, 1968.

Melucci, Alberto. *Nomads of the Present: Social Movements and Individual Needs in Contemporary Society.* Edited by John Keane and Paul Mier. Philadelphia: Temple University Press, 1989.

Mouffe, Chantal. *The Return of the Political.* London: Verson, 1993.

Neufeld, Andrew and Andrew Parnaby. *The IWA in Canada: The Life and Times of an Industrial Union.* Vancouver: IWA Canada/New Star Books, 2000.

O'Brien, James. "The Development of a New Left in the United States, 1960-1965." Ph.D. diss., University of Wisconsin, 1971.

Palmer, Bryan D. *Descent into Discourse: the Reification of Language and the Writing of Social History.* Philadelphia: Temple University Press, 1990.

—. *Solidarity: The Rise and Fall of an Opposition in British Columbia.* Vancouver: New Star Books, 1987.

—. *Working-Class Experience: Rethinking the History of Canadian Labour, 1800-1991.* 2nd ed. Toronto: McClelland and Stewart, 1992.

Parr, Joy and Mark Rosenfeld, eds. *Gender and History in Canada.* Toronto: Copp Clark Ltd, 1996.

Patey, Francis. *A Battle Lost: An Unsuccessful Attempt to Save the Seal Hunt.* Grand Falls, Nfld: Robinson-Blackmore printing and Publishing, 1990.

Przeworski, Adam. *Capitalism and Social Democracy.* Cambridge; New York: Cambridge University Press, 1985.

Rajala, Richard A. *Clearcutting the Pacific Rain Forest: Production, Science, and Regulation.* Vancouver: UBC Press, 1998.

Ryan, Shannon and Larry Small. *Haulin' Rope and Gaff: Songs and Poetry in the History of the Newfoundland Seal Fishery.* St. John's: Breakwater Books, 1978.

Ryan, Shannon. *The Ice Hunters: A History of Newfoundland Sealing to 1914.* St. John's, Nfld: Breakwater, 1994.

Salloch, Roger. *In Pursuit of Ideology: The French Student Revolt, May/June 1968.* Cambridge: Center for International Studies, Massachusetts Institute of Technology, 1969.

Sangster, Joan. *Earning Respect: The Lives of Working Women in Small-Town Ontario 1920-1960.* Toronto: University of Toronto Press, 1985.

Scott, Alan. *Ideology and the New Social Movements.* London; Boston: Unwin Hyman, 1990.

Seeing the Forest Among the Trees: The Case for Holistic Forest Use. Vancouver: Polestar Press, 1991.

Servan-Schreiber, Jean Jacques. *The Spirit of May.* Translated by Ronald Steel. New York: McGraw-Hill Book Company, 1969.

Smelser, Neil J. *The Theory of Collective Behavior.* New York: Free Press of Glencoe, 1963.

Sturmanis, Karl and Dona Sturmanis. *The Greenpeace Book.* Vancouver: Orca Sound Publications, 1978.

Teeple, Gary. *Globalization and the Decline of Social Reform: Into the Twenty-first Century.* 2nd ed. Aurora, Ontario: Garamond Press, 2000.

Tilly, Charles. *From Mobilization to Revolution.* Reading, Mass.: Addison-Wesley Publishing Company, 1978.

Tilly, Charles. *As Sociology Meets History.* New York: Academic Press, 1981.

Touraine, Alaine. *The May Movement Revolt and Reform: May 1968 – The Student Rebellion and Workers' Strikes – the Birth of a Social Movement.* Leonard F. X. Mayhew, trans.. New York: Random House, 1971.

—. *The Voice and Eye: An Analysis of Social Movements.* Alan Duff, trans. Cambridge; New York: Cambridge University Press, 1981.

Touraine, Alaine et al.. *Anti-nuclear protest: The Opposition to Nuclear Energy in France.* Cambridge; New York: Cambridge University Press, 1983.

Wallerstein, Immanuel and Paul Starr. Eds. *The University Crisis Reader: Volume I and II.* New York: Random House, 1971.

Warford, Mark, comp. *Greenpeace: Witness, Twenty-Five Years on the Environmental Front Line.* Andre Deutsch, 1996.

Wilson, Jeremy. *Talk and Log: Wilderness Politics in British Columbia, 1965-96.* Vancouver: UBC Press, 1998.

Wood, Ellen Meiksins. *Democracy Against Capitalism: Renewing Historical Materialism.* Cambridge; New York: Cambridge University Press, 1995.

—. *The Retreat from Class : A New "True" Socialism.* London: Verso, 1986.

Wood, Ellen Meiksins and John Bellamy Foster, eds. *In Defense of History : Marxism and the Postmodern Agenda.* New York: Monthly Review Press, 1997.

Wright, Guy David. *Sons and Seals: A Voyage to the Ice.* St. John's, Nfld: Institute of Social and Economic Research Memorial University of Newfoundland, 1984.

Videos and Radio

Greenpeace. Produced by Anne Hainesworth. 10 min., Magic Lantern, 1995, videocassette.

Weakley, Jeff. *Greenpeace's Greatest Hits.* Produced and directed by Tom Tatum. 60 min., J2 Communications, 1989, videocassette.

Maclear, Michael, and Shelley Saywell. *The Greenpeace Years.* Directed by Shelley Saywell. 55 min., National Film Board of Canada, 1992, videocassette.

"Greenpeace and the Politics of Image" Ideas, CBC Radio Transcripts (9 November 1993).

INDEX